HEDGE WITCHCRAFT

A Beginner Hedge Witch's Guide to Practicing Hedgecraft, with Herbal Magic, Hedge Riding and Trance Methods, Magical Recipes and Spells, and the Hedge Witch's Altar and Tools

LISA CHAMBERLAIN & STACEY CARROLL

Hedge Witchcraft

Copyright © 2023 by Lisa Chamberlain.

All rights reserved. No part of this book may be reproduced in any form without permission in writing from the author. Reviewers may quote brief passages in reviews

Published by **Chamberlain Publications (Wicca Shorts)**

ISBN-13: 978-1-912715-85-5

Disclaimer

No part of this publication may be reproduced or transmitted in any form or by any means, mechanical or electronic, including photocopying or recording, or by any information storage and retrieval system, or transmitted by email without permission in writing from the publisher.

While all attempts have been made to verify the information provided in this publication, neither the author nor the publisher assumes any responsibility for errors, omissions, or contrary interpretations of the subject matter herein.

This book is for entertainment purposes only. The views expressed are those of the author alone, and should not be taken as expert instruction or commands. The reader is responsible for his or her own actions.

Adherence to all applicable laws and regulations, including international, federal, state, and local governing professional licensing, business practices, advertising, and all other aspects of doing business in the US, Canada, or any other jurisdiction is the sole responsibility of the purchaser or reader.

Neither the author nor the publisher assumes any responsibility or liability whatsoever on the behalf of the purchaser or reader of these materials.

Any perceived slight of any individual or organization is purely unintentional.

YOUR FREE GIFT

Thank you for adding this book to your Wiccan library! To learn more, why not join Lisa's Wiccan community and get an exclusive, free spell book?

The book is a great starting point for anyone looking to try their hand at practicing magic. The ten beginner-friendly spells can help you to create a positive atmosphere within your home, protect yourself from negativity, and attract love, health, and prosperity.

Little Book of Spells is now available to read on your laptop, phone, tablet, Kindle or Nook device!

To download, simply visit the following link:

www.wiccaliving.com/bonus

GET THREE FREE AUDIOBOOKS FROM LISA CHAMBERLAIN

Did you know that all of Lisa's books are available in audiobook format? Best of all, you can get **three audiobooks completely free** as part of a 30-day trial with Audible.

Wicca Starter Kit contains three of Lisa's most popular books for beginning Wiccans, all in one convenient place. It's the best and easiest way to learn more about Wicca while also taking audiobooks for a spin! Simply visit:

www.wiccaliving.com/free-wiccan-audiobooks

Alternatively, *Spellbook Starter Kit* is the ideal option for building your magical repertoire using candle and color magic, crystals and mineral stones, and magical herbs. Three spellbooks —over 150 spells—are available in one free volume, here:

www.wiccaliving.com/free-spell-audiobooks

Audible members receive free audiobooks every month, as well as exclusive discounts. It's a great way to experiment and see if audiobook learning works for you.

If you're not satisfied, you can cancel anytime within the trial period. You won't be charged, and you can still keep your books!

CONTENTS

Preface 11

Prologue: Witches in the Hedgerow 14

    Defining the Hedgerow 16
    Medicine, Magic, and the Faery Folk 19
    Portal to the Underworld 22

Introduction 24

Chapter One: The Hedge Witch's Craft 27

    Origins of the Term "Hedge Witch" 30
    What Hedge Witches Do 32
        Animism and the Spirit of Place 35
        A Word to the Wise 36

Chapter Two: Working with Spirit 38

    Types of Spirits 40
        Ancestors 40
        Animal Guides 42
        Elementals 47
        The Fae 48
        Familiars and Fetch Beasts 50
        Deity 52
        Spirit Guides 52

Chapter Three: Hedge Riding 54

The World Tree and the Three Worlds............................. 55
   Underworld.. *56*
   Middleworld... *56*
   Upperworld.. *57*
Skills of Hedge Riding 59
   Protection *59*
   Divination.. *62*
   Astral Projections... *68*
   Shapeshifting... *69*

Chapter Four: Methods of Trance 72

   Drumming *74*
   Chanting.. *74*
   Breathwork... *75*
   Ecstatic Dance *75*
   Music *76*
   Meditation and Visualization... *76*

Chapter Five: The Hedge Witch's Herbal 78

Herbs of the Hedge 79
Herbs of the Hedge Witch – The Banes.......................... 89
Harvesting, Drying, and Storing Herbs........................... 98
   Harvesting.. *99*
   Drying.. *100*
   Storing Herbs... *101*

Chapter Six: Trees of the Hedge Witch.............................. 103

   Alder (Alnus Glutinosa)... *104*
   Apple (Malus Domestica)... *105*
   Ash (Fraxinus Excelsior)... *105*
   Birch (Betula Alba).. *106*

Blackthorn (Prunus Spinosa) 107
Elder (Sambucus Nigra) 108
Hawthorn (Crataegus Monogyna) 109
Oak (Quercus Robur) 110
Rowan (Sorbus Aucuparia) 110
Spindle (Euonymus Europaeus) 111
Willow (Salix Alba) 112
Yew (Taxus Baccata 112

Chapter Seven: Tools of the Hedge Witch 114

Flying Ointment 115
Teas 116
Tinctures 121
Hedge Witch's Bag 122
Rattles and Drums 123
Talismans 125

Chapter Eight: The Hedge Witch's Altar 126

Altar Cover 127
Statuary/Deity Representation 128
Working Surface 128
Elemental Representations 129
Cauldron 130
Stang 130
Besom 131
Trance Aids 132
Hedge Representation 133
Bones and Skulls 133
Green Man/Green Lady 134
Candles 135

Chapter Nine: **Hedge Crossing Ritual** **136**

  The Ritual *137*
  Some Notes *140*

Chapter Ten: **Charms and Recipes of the Hedge Witch** **141**

  Ointments 142
  Simple Ointment Recipe *144*
  Charm Bags 146
  Incenses and Smokes 148
  Oils 150
  Bath Salts 153
  Blessings and Invocations 155

Conclusion **157**

  Suggestions for Further Reading *158*
  About the Authors *160*

PREFACE

Shortly after this book collaboration first got underway, I manifested my dream house. By "dream house" I don't mean some grand mansion with chandeliers and a swimming pool, but instead a small, 1920s bungalow with creaky old hardwood floors, stunning sunlit windows, a yard with built-in garden beds, and plenty of trees in every direction you look—all just a short walk to my favorite bookstore in town.

(In case you're wondering, the manifestation work involved a honey jar spell, a lot of focused visualization, expanding my beliefs about what's possible, and roughly a year of being patient and remaining optimistic!)

One of the first things I noticed when I first came to look at the house was that the yard is bordered on one side by a hedge. This is not exactly common in American neighborhoods—at least not compared to countries like Ireland, where I once lived and traveled for a time.

It might have seemed a fairly trivial detail to me if I hadn't just begun editing this book, but as I stood at the edge of the property, taking in the sight of the house and gardens, and feeling the energies of the land, the hedge seemed like the final punctuation of a message from the

Universe—*this is your new home, and it's been here waiting for you.*

It also felt like a nod of confirmation about this new venture I've been undertaking—collaborating with other writers in the witching world to bring a diversity of topics to a wider audience, and broadening my own horizons while I'm at it. It's so refreshing and inspiring to discover new perspectives and experiences to learn from, and it's my hope that readers will benefit at least as much as I have from this co-creation.

So why hedge witchcraft? To an eclectic witch with heavy leanings to the "green" side, this set of beliefs and practices within the wider world of witchcraft is intriguing to say the least. While "green" and "hedge" are not one and the same path, there is a fair amount of overlap, particularly in the emphasis on herbal magic and medicine, and plenty of witches do incorporate both paths into their practice.

For me, the hedge witch is the quintessential nature witch, gathering magical supplies from the fields, forests, and hedgerows, and communing with the energies of the wilderness. I also appreciate hedge witchcraft's recognition of the various nonphysical energies and beings within the tapestry of the nonphysical realm, or what hedge witches call "Otherworld."

The Three Worlds framework at the center of contemporary hedgecraft is a bit different from my own concepts and experiences of "journeying" into other realms, but it is rooted in ancient wisdom traditions found in many parts of the world, and I'm always fascinated by the common spiritual threads that run through otherwise very different cultures. For me personally, journeying (or multidimensional travel, as I sometimes call it) has only ever made sense in a natural setting, so the metaphor of "crossing the hedge" definitely resonates with my own practice.

I was also intrigued by Stacey Carroll, the co-author of this book, and her website and blog, "The Country Witch's Cottage" (**thecountrywitchscottage.com**). She brings plenty of personal experience with hedge witchcraft to the table, as well as a down-to-earth sensibility and an Australian perspective, which is a nice change of pace in a field largely dominated by writers from the Northern Hemisphere!

Stacey grew up in a postcard-perfect environment for a witch: a stone cottage next to an oak tree in the countryside. I grew up in a rural, heavily wooded area myself. Perhaps there's something about being surrounded by nature at a young age that leads the magically-inclined toward paths like hedge witchcraft and other nature-focused practices.

But of course, it doesn't actually matter where you're from—this path is open to anyone who feels truly called to follow it, whether you're living in the country, the concrete jungle, or somewhere in between.

Besides, no matter where we are, "home" is truly only ever found within. This is a good thing to keep in mind, by the way, when you're journeying beyond the hedge. I wish you safe and fruitful travels.

— Lisa Chamberlain, Editor and Co-author

PROLOGUE: WITCHES IN THE HEDGEROW

For some people, the word "hedgerow" might bring up images of long, orderly rows of tall shrubs lining the country roads in various parts of Europe. For those who love old folk tales and legends, the hedgerow may be a slightly wilder affair, a patch of unkempt wilderness that houses faeries, poison berries, and even (presumably "evil") witches. Indeed, the archetypal hedgerow is a mix of the quaint and the mysterious. But what is a hedgerow, exactly?

For European readers, this might seem like a silly question, but these ancient land enclosures weren't widely used in North America, and most that did exist were lost long ago to industrialized agriculture.

The hedgerow, like much of modern witchcraft, is essentially of European origin, so it isn't part of the cultural subconscious of American witches in the same way it might be for British or Irish practitioners, for example. In fact, the only familiarity most Americans have with hedgerows is probably from Led Zeppelin's song "Stairway to Heaven," in a lyric that many find quite puzzling! ("If there's a bustle in your hedgerow, don't be alarmed now....")

Most of us on this side of the Atlantic are more familiar with the word *hedge*, which usually suggests a domesticated, neat row of single-species box-shaped bushes bordering a yard or lawn.

But a *hedgerow* is something less tame, more interesting, and arguably more energetically potent than the lines of shrubs we see along city sidewalks. With its plants and trees of various shapes and sizes, and its rambling, somewhat "scruffy" appearance, the hedgerow has an aura of mystery—a multidimensional presence that echoes through the myths, stories, and legends it appears in, as if it were a character in its own right.

Of course, the terms "hedge" and "hedgerow" are often used synonymously, as they are throughout this book. Furthermore, as we will see later on, the "hedge" in hedge witchcraft is a metaphor, rather than a physical component of modern practice. (This is good news for those of us who have no access to either hedges or hedgerows!)

However, it's a potent and crucial metaphor, and anyone interested in hedgecraft as a spiritual path would benefit from understanding more about the physical realities of its powerful central symbol.

DEFINING THE HEDGEROW

Hedges are ancient forms of land enclosures in many parts of Northern Europe, with some dating back at least 4,000 years. They were used to mark boundaries and protect the people, livestock, and crops within the enclosure.

The word "hedge" didn't originally mean a kind of plant, but referred to any kind of barrier structure, which could involve ditches, trenches, earthen embankments, and/or stone walls. Some ancient hedges could be hundreds of miles long. Trees and other plantings were often (but not always) incorporated into these hedges.

A *hedgerow*, then, was a hedge consisting solely of trees, shrubs, grasses, and other plants growing close together in a row, which serve as a living fence.

The first hedgerows, formed at least as far back as the Bronze age, were simply strips of woodland left in between fields cleared for growing crops. Later, hedgerows were planted intentionally, and came to serve a number of purposes as they evolved.

In addition to protecting communities and livestock from natural predators, would-be thieves, and warring parties, these lines of vegetation also offered shelter from high winds, shade from the hot sun, wood for kindling and timber, medicinal and culinary herbs, and fruit and nuts to help sustain the people and wildlife alike.

It's doubtful our forebears knew they were creating wildlife refuges for millennia to come, but this is exactly what happened. Today, hedgerows provide crucial habitat for hundreds of species of plant and animal life that would otherwise have disappeared due to population growth and the Industrial Revolution.

They also function as corridors for wildlife to travel between otherwise isolated natural areas. Fortunately, there are now growing movements to preserve existing hedgerows in the UK and Ireland, as well as initiatives to plant new hedgerows in Europe and North America, to restore and promote biodiversity.

For a witch, the hedgerow is a powerful and unique manifestation of the co-creational relationship between humans and nature. What begins as a line of planted shrubs and/or trees becomes its own ecosystem over time, especially in a multi-species hedgerow—the more native species, the better.

The intentional plantings attract birds, insects, and mammals seeking food or shelter. Seeds are deposited by visiting birds or carried in on the wind, where they nestle into the soil under the low branches and grow into herbs, flowers, and even trees. And these plants and trees are home to a host of other life forms, including micro-fungi and moths, which are important to balanced ecosystems.

Some hedgerows have actually been found to have more species of herbs than forests do. Without question, the hedgerow shows us how cooperating with nature benefits *all* species, not just humans and their domesticated animals.

Just as important as these practical considerations, however, is the powerful symbolism of the hedgerow—as the liminal terrain between safety and danger, shelter and exposure, the controlled and the wild, the known and unknown.

Yet the hedgerow was not simply the dividing line between these opposites. It was also its own living entity, teeming with the energies of its inhabitants, from the earthworms, mosses, shrubs, birds, and butterflies to the majestic grace of the oldest, tallest trees in the row.

And of course, it also hosted nonphysical inhabitants—the faeries and nature spirits whose presence can be perceived by witches and other sensitives.

MEDICINE, MAGIC, AND THE FAERY FOLK

A witch living near a hedgerow in centuries past would have found it a very convenient place to forage for medicinal & magical herbs. In fact, all of the herbs named in the old Anglo-Saxon "Nine Herbs Charm" (mugwort, plantain, lamb's cress, nettle, betony, mayweed, crabapple, chervil, and fennel) were found growing either within or alongside the hedgerows.

Of course, many hedge trees and shrubs, such as rowan, oak, hawthorn, and hazel, were also sacred to our pagan ancestors. Oak trees were famously revered by the Druids, for example, and hazelnuts were used in Samhain divination rituals in parts of Scotland. Wands made from hazel, rowan, yew, and other hedge trees were used by Irish Druids and Norse *volur* (or "seeresses") alike. Any of these plants, shrubs, and trees growing in a hedgerow would have been highly valued by witches for physical as well as spiritual uses.

Faeries have always been connected to hedgerows, as we can see from the folklore of Britain and Ireland. Many hedgerow species, like elder, foxglove and nettles, were associated with faeries. It was said that planting holly in the hedge would attract faeries to one's yard. Nettles were markers of faery dwellings, and the hawthorn tree was guardian of the entrance to the faery realm. A hawthorn growing along with ash and oak was a sure sign of faeries in the vicinity, and to this day in Ireland, a hawthorn and blackthorn growing together constitutes a portal to the faeries.

Faeries in the hedgerow were not necessarily good news, however. Much, if not most, of faery lore was centered on avoiding or protecting oneself from their influence. Birch, another hedgerow tree, was carried to prevent kidnapping by the faeries, and rowan was believed to protect against negative faery magic.

Children were warned about the danger of being "spirited away" or made ill by the faeries within the hedgerows if they wandered into the wrong place at the wrong time. Bluebells in particular were to be left undisturbed, as they were flower favorites of the faeries and "ringing the bells" by handling or walking through them might cause the trespasser to be lost in the wilderness until the faeries' spell was broken.

Yet there were also customs of leaving offerings to the faeries, usually in the form of food and drink (such as mead or milk, bread, and butter) or ribbons and coins. This suggests that there was a relationship of mutual understanding between the humans and the faery folk, which could benefit both groups as long as the humans understood who they were dealing with.

Some might even seek the faeries' assistance with a problem or desire, leaving an offering as exchange for their services. In other words, not all faeries were necessarily evil or ill-intentioned (or at least not all of the time), but they had to be respected within their territory—whether in fields, forests, or hedgerows—or trouble would ensue.

Not surprisingly, hedgerow superstitions also extended to witches, who were said to fly along the tops of hedges, and could be prevented from entering one's property if holly trees were planted within the row. Yet, as we will see later on, the general fear of witches in those days didn't prevent people from seeking their assistance when someone was ill or suspected they were under a curse and wanted it lifted. (There's a certain irony about the fact that the desired assistance often involved herbs from the hedgerows that the people didn't want witches traipsing around in!)

This paradox of belief is also reflected in magical lore around hedgerow plants themselves. While bluebells were dangerous due to their faery associations (and possibly due to their toxicity to humans), they also could be used for magic related to love and honesty. Primrose was hung over windows on Beltane, a time when the veil is thin, to block dark magic but allow white magic into the house—suggesting that primrose held the protective, barrier-like energy of the hedgerow as a whole.

The hedgerow held both danger and beneficial potential, both magically and practically. It contained sustenance and medicine as well as thorns and poison. Sometimes medicine and poison co-existed within the same plant (as we will see in the discussion of baneful herbs in chapter 5).

PORTAL TO THE UNDERWORLD

Whether or not a given folk belief had any basis in what we might call "ordinary reality," the lore as a whole points to the hedgerow as a gateway to an extraordinary reality, a quality of energy that can still be felt within and around hedgerows—or any natural place—today.

This energy manifests as both a stillness and a presence, creating a place where time can cease to exist, as one simply experiences the living beings (both visible and invisible) around them. One hedge species that particularly embodies this timeless, magical energy is the continually regenerating yew tree, said by the Celts to have come to Ireland from the Otherworld itself.

Spending time in close examination of the diversity of life thriving within a proper hedgerow will reveal all kinds of details that you wouldn't see if you simply glanced at the row while walking by.

What begins as a nondescript patch of leaves and branches suddenly becomes an entire world unto itself, where every square inch is alive with growing, fluttering, crawling, flitting and buzzing beings—each small yet crucial manifestation adds something to a powerful, integrated and magical whole. The Otherworld is similarly hidden, surprising, mysterious, and interconnected, yet it is all around us, and entirely accessible to those who seek it.

From a human perspective, hedgerows may be largely a thing of the past (except for those lucky enough to live in areas where they still grow). From the perspective of the natural world, however, the hedgerow illustrates the timeless process of growth, death, and rebirth, and the infinite possibilities of the co-creational energies of the universe.

For the hedge witch, the hedgerow is the perfect symbol of the liminal space between the physical and nonphysical realms, as well as a source of magical herbs, trees, and flowers with which to access the nonphysical world and create change from that limitless space.

Again, you don't need to be physically present in an actual hedgerow to do this. As you will see in the following pages, hedge witchcraft is accessible to any witch who feels truly called toward this path.

In this book, you will learn about the core beliefs and practices of the hedge witch, the various nonphysical beings you may meet on your Otherworld journeys, and basic tools and methods for journeying. You'll also discover magical lore and uses for a host of hedge plants and trees, many of which are likely to be available nearby. Finally, there are hedgecraft recipes and other resources for taking your next steps along the path of the hedge witch. So enjoy all the magical discoveries you are about to make!

INTRODUCTION

Once upon a time I was a young witchlet exploring her power. I embraced the beginning path of Wicca, and from there began devouring every bit of information I could possibly find on the path of witchcraft and being a witch. I was of the generation who had their first introduction to witchcraft from the movie '*The Craft.*' (Yes, I know—I imagine there are a few eye rolls happening right now, but I was a 90's pre-teen and teenager and it was **THE** movie for my generation!)

I also grew up watching *Charmed*, *Sabrina*, *Practical Magic* and *Buffy,* so the idea of witches and magic was quite prevalent in my childhood. To be fair, we were spoiled for choice during that decade. However, there were a lot of conflicting ideas about witchcraft presented within these shows and movies, and as a voracious reader and knowledge hound, I was determined to find the truth of it all and know what was what.

While exploring my path and trying different things, I could never really grasp the idea of ceremonial magic—all the trappings of wands, athames, chalices and crystal balls. I was a very simple witch at the heart of it. I liked herbs and candles, and I preferred to read cards and sit by our oak tree, sharing energy and seeking its wisdom.

I liked creating things with my hands and growing plants. I sought the company of the outdoors and the things that roamed the in-between places while I tried to sleep. I could see the shapes and beings that sat on the other side of the veil, waiting for an audience or acknowledgment. Some nights I would see the strangest things; other times I would hear voices or smell scents that were not part of my every day routine. It began to make me wonder, and before long I discovered a term that seemed to sum up my spiritual life quite easily:

Hedge Witch.

It was rather strange the way I came across the term. I wasn't looking for it at all. I was just doing my usual searching on the internet for information and came across the term in a blog. From there I began to read, research, and apply the practice of hedge witchcraft, and it became clear that this was my natural path, the path that had all along been the one for me.

There are so many different interpretations of hedge witchcraft, there is not one single handbook that will give you direct steps to becoming a hedge witch. Many variations, ideologies, interpretations and ways of experiencing hedge witchcraft are presented in books, articles, blogs and vlogs.

Hedge witchcraft has many areas of study to learn and master, and it can require sacrifice and strength. It is a beautiful path that will challenge and test you to make sure you are committed, but ultimately it will help you grow in many ways, bringing many different facets of your experience together to create a path unique to you.

This book will provide a working roadmap to help you build your practice as a hedge witch. But it is my hope that this book helps you build a strong foundation for exploring the ever-changing and evolving path of hedge witchcraft in a modern world.

Chapter One: THE HEDGE WITCH'S CRAFT

*"There she stands with herbs in her hair, muttering words that no man knows.
Watch and see how the trees bend to her will;
They know she speaks secrets only a few know"*

—S. Carroll

Picture a cottage in the middle of the forest surrounded by all manner of trees, plants and herbs; smoke curls from the chimney while a wicked potion brews upon the fire. Herbs hang from the ceiling, some familiar, some not, in a cacophony of scent permeating the very earth on which the home stands. There are jars everywhere filled with wonders that seem to be beyond this world; magic vibrates from this place as though in a fairy tale—the home of the story's witch.

It's an evocative image, and for some witches, true enough to what life as a witch is like. But in recent times there has been a trend of romanticizing the idea of what a hedge witch is and how a hedge witch lives: the intriguing "fairy tale" witches who know things others don't, who can command nature and have access to mystical knowledge that mere mortals could never dream of.

The truth is far less glamorous and somewhat mundane. A hedge witch is a witch like any other, to a point. You will find them in cities, in the countryside, in apartments, houses, and cottages, working in banks, in the supermarket, at the doctor's office and in your local garden center.

Witchcraft is rarely lucrative, so most witches have other jobs that pay the bills. Yes, there are some lucky witches who have been able to leverage their craft into a full-time job by opening a store or online business, doing readings, and performing spell work, but most of us have normal careers.

Hedge witchcraft is its own path, but it is a highly individualized path a lot of the time. The old adage "ask ten different witches what witchcraft is and you will get ten different answers" definitely applies here. There is no set way of being a hedge witch. There are elements of the practice that we all share, but like any other witchcraft path, we create and build our own as we go.

What I can tell you for certain is that hedge witchcraft is not green/cottage/kitchen witchcraft, nor is it herbalism. I will not deny that hedge witchcraft encompasses some of the ideology and practices within those particular traditions—after all, most witchcraft is adaptive and inclusive—but it is not one of those in and of itself. It stands alone as its own individual practice and tradition.

If hedge witchcraft is not green, cottage, or kitchen witchcraft, then what exactly is it?

Hedge witchcraft is a path with many overlapping historical and folkloric roots. Within the lore and traditions of hedge witchery, you will see patterns of shamanism from the Celtic, Anglo Saxon and Greek worlds. Practices that stemmed from those periods include communing with spirits, divining the future, storytelling, and working with herbs. These practices are intimately wrapped up in hedgecraft, creating a beautiful, intricate and powerful path that combines working with the Earth with the more shamanic elements of trance, healing, and spirit work.

ORIGINS OF THE TERM "HEDGE WITCH"

While often thought to be a modern term, "hedge witch" has its roots in our ancestors and their practices. If you look throughout time, you will see terms used to describe folk magic practitioners and healers that were the forbearers of this practice. "Druid" and "shaman" are obviously well-known terms that we associate with ancient spiritual practices, but they are not all that existed.

The term "hedge witch" has its etymological roots in the Saxon word *haegtessa,* translating to "hedge rider," meaning "one who moves between worlds" or "one who straddles the hedge." We also see in the old Germanic tongue the word *hagzusa* and the middle Dutch *haghetisse* (quite close to the Saxon) all referring to "hedge witch" or "hedge rider." As these peoples migrated and branched out into different parts of the world, they brought these words and practices with them.

The hedge within the term "hedge witchcraft" comes from the hedges that would border a town in the old days, protecting it from wild creatures and predators that lay beyond the borders. The hedge would keep in livestock, protect the farm and the farmer's family, and protect the village as a whole. Generally, people didn't much venture beyond their own small towns back then. Generations upon generations would live in the same town, within the same hedged borders, and continue the traditions and practices of their families.

The folk healers and wise women of the village often lived at the very edge of these borders or just beyond them, working their charms, spells, healing and hex work. They were both feared and respected for their abilities. Because they lived so close to the border, they were often perceived as the ones who could cross the border and come back unscathed, with knowledge and gifts that couldn't be explained. This gave birth to the idea of these men and women being "other," and from there the ideas and practices of modern hedge witchcraft were born.

WHAT HEDGE WITCHES DO

*A tenth I know: when at night the witches
ride and sport in the air,
such spells I weave that they wander home
out of skins and wits bewildered...*

— *Hávamál*, "The Song of Spells," 154

Hedge witches work with spirits, herbs, divination and the elements; working in many ways to heal, and discover information. They work with one foot in this world and one foot in the Otherworld by straddling the hedge. From this stance, the hedge witch can perform many different tasks, spells, rituals, works and divinations that can have an effect in both worlds.

In the truest sense, the hedge in hedge witchcraft is not actually a physical hedge—it is the metaphysical barrier between our world and Otherworld, the astral realms and the Spirit world. Hedge riding is the art of slipping the skin in trance and traveling to Otherworld: a witch will "ride" the hedge to the desired location, often assisted by an animal spirit or by shapeshifting into an animal form to better navigate Otherworld.

Think of Circe, Pasiphae and Medea from Greek mythology. All are thought to be powerful sorceresses and Priestesses of Hecate, who is a crossroad Deity or Gatekeeper to Otherworld. Circe and Medea both worked with poisonous herbs taught from the garden of Hecate – herbs associated with witchcraft and flying ointments.

Circe was adept at shapeshifting others through her magic, and was possibly quite able to shapeshift herself. Medea and Pasiphae were both very adept in the art of poisons, potions and herbs. Their stories show that the practice of working with herbs, potions, spirits and magic was very much part of the ancient world.

Elsewhere, the Norse had volvas, women who were powerful seeresses and shamans. They practiced the art of seidr, a form of trance work used to obtain answers to questions, to perform magic, and to learn the course of fate. Scotland had their spaewives – women who would work with prophecy, healing and dreams. In Ireland there are tales of the bean feasa; wise women who healed and would contact Otherworld in order to determine the cause of an issue and how to cure it. All of these paths and practices are very reminiscent of the hedge witch practice.

Although hedge witchcraft is not the same thing as herbalism, hedge witches often functioned as healers or herbalists in their villages when doctors were not available or too expensive. A simple remedy to heal an ailment was one of the arts that a hedge witch would have been well versed in.

Folk healers and folk magic practitioners were also known in some regions as "cunning folk" and "wise women." They were what you might think the medieval witch would be, but the role was not limited to women—both men and women could be thought of as cunning folk.

Perhaps one of the more famously known cunning folk was an Irish woman by the name of Biddy Early. Biddy is well known throughout Ireland and the British Isles. At one point in her life she was even accused of witchcraft, but she was so well respected that no one would speak out against her.

Biddy was a healer and worked with traditional remedies that she had learned from her own mother. It is said that Biddy would speak with faeries and was incredibly intuitive, able to discern the exact illness of a person and determine a course of action. She was said to carry a blue bottle with her that had a dark liquid in it, which she would often consult to determine what possible cure the sick person may need.

From the early medieval period to the twentieth century, cunning folk and wise women were considered to be semi-professional folk (or low) magic practitioners. While not always a full-time profession, cunning work could pay for food and housing, and often practitioners would barter services for things they needed.

They worked to remove curses or the evil eye, heal spiritual woes as well as physical ones with herbs and charms, and even act as midwives. Most were important people in their community; often the normal lay person could not afford a doctor, so they would go to the local cunning person or wise woman for help. Oddly enough, cunning folk would get a lot of work to undo alleged malefic witchcraft work, yet the Church thought of cunning folk as being in league with the Devil.

Cunning folk and wise women were much attuned to their surroundings; they had to be in order to be successful because most of their product would come from the land around them. They would know how to work in concert with the spirits that lived in their area and the spirits that lived within the tools that they used. Likewise, as a hedge witch, you will most likely find yourself leaning into animism and understanding the spirit of place, and the spirit within all things.

ANIMISM AND SPIRIT OF PLACE

Animism, from the latin word *anima* (meaning spirit or life) is a term used to describe the belief that all things have a spirit. To see things with an animistic viewpoint is to see things as soul or spirit and not just as matter. The rocks, the trees, the flowers, the dirt—everything that surrounds you—has life and purpose. To work with the natural world is to work with the spirits that live within all things.

Have you ever touched a tree or worked with a plant and felt that it had an energy all its own that wanted to interact with you? Many books on witchcraft teach that when you harvest from a plant, it is customary to leave some sort of offering. This is because of the belief that within the plant is a spirit or soul, an energy that provides its own power. When you connect with nature you will begin to feel the spirit in all things; it is necessary and important in order to do your work and do it well.

Hedge witchcraft also involves an inherent belief that *places* also have souls or spirits of their own. There is a gorge near where I live, situated between two mountains. The mountains aren't particularly large, but they're impressive, and when you drive the road between them you can feel the spirit of the mountain watching you, assessing.

It is an unnerving experience when a spirit of a land as ancient as my own is putting out feelers. The best way I can describe it is like a huge pressure between the ears; it's unlike anything I have ever felt. But I understand there are spirits that live within this land that have reason to be suspicious or watchful of those who traverse it.

Each landscape will have soul or spirit to it—even urban jungles. It is easier to feel and connect with the spirit of place, or the *genius loci,* when it is an open field, an ancient monument or standing stones, or even a forest because there is an uninterrupted quality to it. But if the urban jungle is where you feel strongest, it is always possible to connect with the spirit of that place and work with it.

A WORD TO THE WISE

Hedgecraft is not the easiest path to walk, especially if you are gifted when it comes to spirit work and prophecy. You will find that it can be difficult, downright frightening, and on occasion, painful. Traversing other realms is not something that you can do for light fun or because you are bored, nor is it something you should do because it sounds trendy. It's a serious undertaking that shouldn't be taken lightly.

Witchcraft is not a band-aid or cure-all for what ails you in life. Sometimes the best thing you can do is follow a mundane path to your desires. However, witchcraft is a valuable tool in giving those mundane actions a big kick into gear. I wouldn't say magic doesn't provide miracles or that Spirit doesn't provide the way, but you also can't expect it to fall into your lap if you don't do the work in the physical plane to give it a pathway toward you.

Hedge witchcraft is a powerful road to walk, one you have to be ready for. It causes you to bleed, to cry, to find yourself and discover the hidden depths of your inner world. It is something you live daily. It can't be turned off because it is who you are, not just something you do.

You become the spirit walker, the mystic, the healer, the wild one, the secret one. You dance to a different drum, seeing the world differently, inhabiting the world differently. The idea of normalcy changes. It requires much (and for some, too much) but if you have a brave spirit and strong soul, and a passion for herb-lore and beasts and spirits of the wild, you may just find the hedge witchcraft path is for you.

Chapter Two: WORKING WITH SPIRIT

One of the most important parts of hedge witchcraft is working with Spirit. Hedge witches journey to the other side to commune with Spirit, to learn information and bring it back with them in order to give guidance, share prophetic information, healing, spell work and messages.

Working with Spirit is not an easy path, nor is it for everyone. Sometimes the experience can be very intense and confusing. Communing with spirits can be hard, because they are not always willing to be straightforward or helpful. Sometimes you are told what you need to hear instead of what you want to hear. A lot of the time they will supply you with clues or riddles to encourage you to look for the answers yourself, and with that seeking comes growth.

Spirit also does not operate on our time—they will not hurry up just because you want them to. It is often said that Spirit works outside of our own concept of time. Because Spirit is "Other" and exists in a different realm to us, what is urgent on our plane may not seem to be urgent on their plane.

Yet Spirit can provide an immense magical boost to your workings and enhance your knowledge while you practice. Once you begin cultivating a relationship with Spirit, you will see strides of improvement, growth, and synchronicity in your ritual, spell craft and everyday life.

Take the time to learn about the various kinds of spirits within the realm of Spirit, and how they can assist you. Feed your spirits, give them offerings, find out what gives them strength, and don't abuse them to further your aims. Approach them with a balanced attitude, a willingness to grow together, and a clear idea of what you need from the spirit and what you can provide in return.

TYPES OF SPIRITS

Below are some examples of spirits or beings that you may come across when you begin hedge riding.

This is by no means a comprehensive list, but it is a good starting point for recognizing and understanding the spirits you may encounter, or approach to build a working relationship with, when journeying through Otherworld.

ANCESTORS

Ancestors are an important part of who we are; they are our blood, our entire reason for existing. Who we are is generations of relationships that go back to when your family line began. But before we get too far into Ancestor work and how they can assist you on your journey, it is important to point out that you are not required to forgive or be kind to your ancestors just because they are your ancestors, if there are past issues with them.

If you are willing to resolve those issues, then working with your ancestors can be a great way to do so; but bear in mind that if your ancestor was a particularly nasty or toxic person, it is doubtful this has changed with their death. You are not required to offer automatic forgiveness or entry to your space to ancestors that have caused harm, are harmful or will create havoc. Another note too, just because they are your ancestor does not mean that they wish you well. Regardless of family ties it is very important to be discerning as to who you let into your sacred space or journey with.

Ancestors, outside of the aforementioned situations, will often be your biggest champions and your source of strength. You are, to them, the current living culmination of all of their blood, sweat, tears and lives. Often ancestors will want to support you, offer guidance and help you in any way they can to improve your life, protect you and guide you.

That being said, they aren't expecting to do that out of sheer love or kindness; feeding your ancestors is a key part of giving them the strength to help you. Ancestors will feed on the energy of food, beverages, plants and incense, just like you require sustenance to live, so do they. You do not have to be elaborate in your offerings; often the gesture is enough, but if you wish them to help you more often and with greater frequency, you may have to up your offerings game.

A simple way to honor and work with your ancestors is to give them their own space. If you can't give them a whole altar to themselves, then a small area of your sacred space purely for them will be fine. Dress their space with a simple white cloth; white is a very neutral color and denotes spirituality. If your ancestral traditions are filled with vibrant colors then by all means, add those.

Keeping it simple to start with is a good idea: a glass of fresh water, a candle, incense, fresh flowers if they are available to you, and any items that were important to your ancestors can be placed on the altar. Offerings can be kept quite simple too: incense, a cup of hot coffee or tea and/or alcohol make very powerful offerings.

Boundaries are an important part of working with your ancestors. You may find yourself having to negotiate what you are and are not willing to do or offer. Your ancestors may want cigars, cigarettes, particular alcohol or food to help manifest their energy more powerfully in our realm. If this is something you can't or won't offer, you will have to work this out with your ancestral spirits. There has to be give and take in order for it to be a successful relationship, and you will both have to come to an agreement as to what you find acceptable or not.

Your ancestors can be invoked or invited into your space when hedge crossing to offer protection, guidance in Otherworld, or to simply watch over you as you begin exploring other realms. They will be vested in your successful return from your journeying and will want to share in your experience. Ancestors are valuable to our work, and if you put in the time and effort in order to build that relationship, you will find your endeavors quite fruitful.

ANIMAL GUIDES

Animal guides are one of the first spiritual connections we will experience as witches, not just as hedge witches but when exploring our spirituality generally. It has become quite trendy to embrace the concept of animal guides without truly understanding their purpose or power when working with Spirit or magic.

Unfortunately, there has also been a misguided trend to refer to animal guides as animal *totems*, but totems are sacred to Native Americans. With this in mind, I refer to them as animal guides as that is what they are—animals who guide us on our journeys.

There are many different animals in the world that can appear to you as your guide; and there is no shame if your guide is a mouse, nor are you more powerful or better if your guide is a lion. Often the spirit of the guide will appear to us in a form that has a lesson for us or could be an important part of our journey.

My guide has remained the same since I was a child but as I explored my spiritual path, others have come to me and I work with each one differently. It is also not unusual to have more than one; each one brings a strength to our practice and an energy that we may need. Guides may also provide you with the means in which to shapeshift into them during your travels, which will be covered in more detail in Chapter 3.

A simple way to divine what kind of animal your guide may be is to look for signs or symbols that are out of the ordinary. While it can be easy to tell yourself that a particular animal is your guide because you always see it, sometimes a crow is just a crow.

If you live in an area with a high concentration of that particular fauna, chances are it's not your animal guide. If you find yourself dreaming about a particular animal all of the time, this is likely your animal guide trying to get your attention. If nothing out of the ordinary is happening, a simple meditation to find your animal guide will reveal the answer – YouTube has some really great and non-complex guided meditations for this, so it is very easy to find one that will assist you.

Let's look at some of the more common animal guides that may present themselves to you and what it could mean if one is your guide:

Bear: Bear is a guardian spirit and will often appear during times of stress or when you are needing extra strength. Bear will teach you to be grounded and connected to the wild aspects of your nature. Bear will guide you toward your own innate power and provide stability while you explore that power.

Crow: The crow may speak to your ability to be a psychopomp. Do you see spirits? Does your magic manifest quickly and successfully? Crow may be your guide in order to help you grow spiritually and find your calling. Embrace your inner wisdom and continue to learn; there is much of the mystic in you waiting to be let out.

Eagle: Are you working toward freedom or dreaming of flying at great heights? Eagle will help you work toward your goals and achieve great things. It is a master predator, able to discern the best course of action to ensure success in its hunts. Eagle is also a powerful symbol of going places, of making the effort to go further than you can ever dream of.

Fish: Fish, especially salmon, can teach you how to win against adversity, how to work with others and to come together to meet collective goals. It will also caution you against going the way of everyone else just because everyone else is. Salmon will swim upstream, facing all sorts of adversity in order to get to where they need to be –

in life, sometimes you will have plenty of challenges before you get to where you need to be.

Fox: Feeling cunning or needing to blend in? Fox can be there to show you how to move through life stealthily and without drawing too much attention.

Horse: Majestic, noble and with a great deal of stamina, horse may teach you how to move through life with grace, endurance and a little bit of whimsy. Horses are all about power and the ability to cover a lot of ground in a short space of time; giving you a much-needed boost on your journey.

Lion: If you are someone who often finds yourself in difficult circumstances, a lion guide will show you how to overcome adversity and thrive in many different situations. Lion will show you how to garner your strength and will also give you strength as you go about your life.

Mouse: Even from the smallest perspective, you will see the larger picture. If you think that your world is only a small place, mouse will show you that there is so much more. While mouse can often end up as prey, mouse will show you how to get around without being noticed, how to make the most of what you have and how to seek out new places in order to help you grow.

Owl: A quick, quiet predator with a history of magical associations, an owl guide will teach you to connect with your intuition and insight, help you to learn keen observation and work with your shadow self. Owl will help you work on your perception and to see the bigger picture before making any hasty decisions. If you watch an owl in the wild, it has patience. It will sit and watch the smallest prey, waiting for the right moment to strike, maximizing its success.

Rabbit: Happiness and expressing the feelings that give you the most joy are important in your life; if you are not doing this enough, rabbit may be there to show you that it is okay to let go and be joyful. Learn to move quickly toward your goals and opportunities to make the most of your life.

Rat: Vermin to some, dirty to others. Yet rat is a powerful symbol of overcoming adversity and showing quick thinking in the face of challenging situations. Rats have a knack for being able to survive and thrive in almost any climate. A rat guide is nothing to dismiss. Rat will show you how to thrive in any situation, using ingenuity and perseverance to succeed.

Snake: Transformation is your key, as the snake is about transformation and adaptability. If snake is your guide; you may be required to undergo tremendous growth and change before you can see some real results in your life.

Spider: You have the ability to weave your own fate and the patience to do it justice. Each strand strung together creates the fabric of your life, your security and your safe haven. But in order to get there, you need to embrace patience. If you feel as though your life lacks meaning, a spider guide will show you that you have the power to weave the life you want and find the meaning you need.

Whale: Majestic and laid back, a whale guide will often teach you how to be in harmony with your surroundings, and to embrace your emotions, intuition and inner voice. If you find yourself swimming in the depths with whale, it will show you how to embrace quiet and solitude whilst exploring the vast depths of yourself.

Wolf: The ultimate in solitude and natural connectedness, a wolf is a symbol of strength, adaptability and regeneration. Wolves are also about family and connections. Wolves are often the balance in nature; a wolf guide may suggest that you are not balanced and ignoring connections, and will help you grow and empower them.

ELEMENTALS

As the elements are an important part of hedgecraft, you may find when journeying that you meet or connect with Elementals. Each element has a creature or being, known as an elemental, that works in concert with it. Each elemental has its own strengths and abilities, as does each of the elements. If you find yourself in Otherworld needing a boost from the elements, an elemental is who you will call on or may come in to support you.

Gnomes are the strength and stability of earth; when you see a gnome the word that comes to mind is *earthy*. They toil away, keeping the bedrock of this world and the next together, making sure things flourish and grow. Gnomes keep earthly matters balanced and do not take kindly to any sort of abuse toward the Earth. Gnomes are also protective; we often place gnomes in our garden to protect it, decorate it and invite in the spirits of nature to tend our patch of earth. Gnomes assist us with stability, strength, being grounded and connecting to plant spirits.

Salamanders are the spirits of Fire; lizard-like in appearance, they are the flickers that dance within the flame as you work with candles or bonfires. When infernos rage, salamanders are at work. When the smallest flickering illuminates the darkest of corners, salamanders are offering a small door to see the way. They can burn with the most amazing intensity or offer a small warmth to warm the soul without the burning heat of a fire. Never take salamanders for granted and always remember them in your works; for as in this world, Otherworld is also made from the elements. Salamanders assist us with our passions, our purpose and the fire within our souls that guide us every day.

Sylphs are the elementals of air—the gentle breeze or the forceful hurricane. They flow through the air, moving it around, dancing in and out of the clouds, bringing rain or parting for the bright sun. They are the ballet in a beautiful dance, the leaf blowing around in a frenzy in the wind, the bird zooming through the air in a colorful flurry of feather and plume. Sylphs assist us with clear thinking, communication, spirit work and clairvoyance.

Undines are the creatures of the deep blue sea, the rambling creeks and the raging rivers. Undines are the singing siren, the playful mermaid, the spirit of the water rushing, pushing, creating change wherever it flows. Undines assist us with clarity, emotional balance, psychic revelations, deep inner work that requires us to be honest with ourselves, and learning to be more in touch with our empathy and compassion without being pushovers.

THE FAE

Is there a spirit or being that evokes more romantic notions and fascinations than that of the Fae? Romantic ballads, epic poetry, folk stories and cautionary tales have been told about the Fae since the dawn of time. From the sweet tales of little gossamer-winged faeries to the darker stories of Fae kidnapping and changelings, faeries have long fascinated the mind and aroused our curiosity.

There are countless tomes written on the history of the Fae; a simple search will turn up plenty of books to flesh out your knowledge with many different perspectives and experiences of working with the Fae, if you wish to create or further a relationship with them.

The Fae aren't all love and light and gossamer wings though; history has shown us they can be quite dark and less than pleasant. As with the human world, the Fae has many types, many personalities and many different behaviors. This is why it's often advised, if you cross into the Fae realm, not to eat or drink their food because you will never find your way home.

There are tales throughout history of faery changeling babies – babies that were switched with perfectly healthy human babies by Fae. This was often thought to be the culprit when children suddenly changed their behavior or fell ill. So as you can see, they are not always the fun, pleasant nature sprites we'd like them to be. When approaching the Fae, always do so with caution and respect; always understand the terms of any agreements and never accept anything from them without knowing the cost.

FAMILIARS AND FETCH BEASTS

There is a fairly consistent argument in the Pagan community about what a familiar is. One side argues that it is any animal that comes into your life when you are practicing and seems to fit the bill of a magical familiar. The other side argues that a familiar is a spirit that works with you, and when its purpose is done, it moves on.

The idea of a familiar being an actual physical animal is from the time of the witch hunts and inquisitions, when the appearance of an animal in the home or near the person being accused denoted that the person was in fact a witch. Many a person who was suspected of being a witch (or accused of being one in order to get them out of someone else's way) simply had a pet cat, dog, or other animal.

A familiar is a protector spirit that works with you and shields you from any and all magical attacks or negative entities or energies. I do not think that as a witch you should assign that particular load to your pet. If a familiar is there to take the hit for us should it become necessary, do you really want to cause that kind of energetic damage or disruption to a living breathing animal?

Animals can be magical assistants or companions when you are at your altar, reading cards, or doing other magical work; generally, familiars are spirits that work in concert with you until the desired objective is achieved.

The term "fetch" originates in Irish folklore, where it referred to the apparition (or double) of a living person, but it has different meanings in witchcraft. There are several different schools of thought on what constitutes a fetch or fetch beast, as it is sometimes known:

- The fetch is a separate entity that comes to us during our lifetime to assist us but is more than a familiar in that it has been with us since our birth and will remain so until our death.

- The fetch is the shadow self or soul that removes itself from us like a second skin and moves into the ether to do our work for us.

- The fetch is the second skin that witches project into when hedge riding.

- The fetch is a spirit entity that accompanies us on our journey, working with us, living within us until such time as it comes out of the body to do its work.

The fetch can be thought of as your second skin, or the skin of yourself in the astral realm. Its form can be seen in this physical realm by someone who is gifted with second sight or mediumship ability. It is with you from the day you are born and will seek you out when the time is right. If you go looking for your fetch, you may not find it. Fetch beasts are shapeshifters; they can come to you as a puff of smoke, a person, an animal, even a dragon. The purpose of the fetch is to work magic with you and carry your wishes out into the ether to help them come to fruition.

Like any spirit, in order to get the best out of your relationship with it, you must feed it and care for it so that it will be able to help you on your journeying.

DEITY

Deity are a form of Spirit. I believe personally that Deities are independent forms that are singular in nature – by this I mean that Diana is not Artemis, Aphrodite is not Venus.

Working with Deity is a delicate dance; you can seek them out and ask for their assistance, but there is no guarantee they will help you if it doesn't suit their purposes. Gods are much like us in the sense that they have their failings, desires, needs, and temperamental moments. Loki the trickster might assist you, but he may also make it come back and bite you if he feels like it.

When approaching Deity for help in Otherworld – or this world – be humble, but don't be a pushover. I'm not suggesting you get on your knees and bow down to them; but don't expect them to do what you wish just because you are asking it. Oftentimes you may even find that if your need or your wish resonates with Deity, they may even approach you, offering a deal or trade-off for their assistance.

If you don't feel comfortable you are free to refuse them, but bear in mind they can sometimes be very pushy when they want something. You may have to be quite firm in your refusal, but stay polite. No sense in ticking off a God if you don't need to.

SPIRIT GUIDES

Perhaps the most well-known and well-loved of all spirit entities that can assist magically is the spirit guide. We all have them. We don't all have a connection to them or know who they are, but they are often there watching over us, making sure we aren't led too astray.

Your spirit guide is there to offer guidance, support your spiritual endeavors and help you fulfill your soul contract. Spirit guides can be animals, angels, ancestors, or other spirits that have found themselves as our guardians. Some people might find that their guides are family members or friends who have passed on, but for other, they're people we've never known.

It is said that your energy picks your guide before you incarnate; however, sometimes spirit guides are simply energy that resonates with us and works toward helping us fulfill our purpose in this lifetime.

Chapter Three:
HEDGE RIDING

Shedding the skin and slipping into the cool night air; flying across skies. Oh what freedom! What joy to experience wonders no mere mortal can conceive of. There is a world beyond this one filled with wonders, horrors, and the wisdom of the ages. You can seek out the far corners of the Universe and see with your spirit what the eyes cannot.

Unfortunately, due to the romanticizing of hedge witchcraft, the harder part of learning to cross properly and walk different realms is often glossed over or ignored, and it does a disservice to the witch who is serious about learning hedgecraft.

Hedge riding is an intense experience. It takes you to other places that you may have previously only dreamt of. Nothing is closed; where you can imagine your spirit soaring is where you will find yourself going. But it helps to have a map of sorts, so we will now look at an ancient spiritual framework used by many hedge witches today.

THE WORLD TREE AND THE THREE WORLDS

The World Tree is a motif found in many cultures that shows a connection between the heavens, the Earth plane, and the underworld. Yggdrasil, the Norse World Tree, is perhaps the most famous of them all. It is said to be a large and sacred Ash (*Fraxinus* genus), although some scholars argue that it could also be a Yew (*Taxus baccata*).

The top of the World Tree sits above the heavens, the trunk inhabits our own world, and the roots reach deep into underworld. It makes sense that the connection between realms would be a tree, which to ancient peoples probably seemed quite magical as it inhabited different realms, grew abundantly, and gave them much of their shelter, shade and sustenance.

There are three parts to the World Tree that correspond to Otherworld: Upperworld, Middleworld and Underworld. While you may journey to other places and realms throughout your hedge witch journey, more often than not you will journey to the three worlds to get to the other places or do your work.

UNDERWORLD

Within various religious traditions, there is an alluding to an underworld of some sort: Christians have their Hell, the Greeks and Romans have Tartarus, the Egyptians had Duat.

Yet the Underworld in hedge witchcraft is not typically a place that is made up of suffering or punishment. Underworld is often a pleasant place to visit, running wild with primal power and all sorts of spirits and entities in something of a pristine environment. Often, this is where your animal guide will reside, or be waiting for you when you hedge cross. It has its darker places like any world but this is probably the place you will journey to most often.

You may seek out spirits, respite for your soul, or connect with Fae, Elementals or other beings that dwell within the Earth. Underworld holds a deeply transformative power. It can show you the way toward your own inner shadow, share with you the connections between souls and energy, and give you a pathway to work on your Self, spirit, and personal healing.

MIDDLEWORLD

Middleworld is our world: Earth, the mundane, the place where you will do more practical-style workings that involve your everyday life.

You will likely see everything normal that you would see in waking life, but you will also see the spirit of things: the spirit of place and the different energy fields, realms and layers that exist within our world. You may also find that you commune with spirits that are existing on this plane for whatever reason and have not yet crossed into Underworld or other lands of the Dead.

Fair warning; if you are spiritually gifted or a medium, you may find yourself shanghaied into being a psychopomp and escorting the souls of the Dead to wherever they are meant to be going. It is a good idea to set your boundaries before traversing Middleworld, especially if you don't particularly want to find yourself becoming a ferryman.

Much like the Underworld, you will be able to perform healing, magical work, divination and converse with beings, entities and spirits that reside within the frequency of Middleworld.

UPPERWORLD

Upperworld is the celestial world: the world of our ancestors, Deities, angels, spirit guides and other heavenly bodies. This is the realm where you would journey to see an overview of your life, to travel to the past, present and future in order to learn about yourself, the greater world and your place in it.

Upperworld could be compared to the Greek Elysian Fields, the Summerland of Wicca, the Tir na nÓg or Mag Mell of the Irish, or other lands in mythology that speak of sunlight, peace, paradise or bliss. Upperworld is also a signifier of the culmination of your journey: traversing Underworld where you face your shadow allows you to grow spiritually, and moving into Middleworld where you face the things in your everyday life that stress you, hurt you or otherwise cause you issues.

Once you have faced those trials, you are ready to move to Upperworld where all will be revealed—your purpose, your journey, your history and your future. While this describes more of a shamanic view of working your way through the three worlds, it's also true in hedge witchcraft. While you may do more work in Underworld or even Middleworld, you will eventually find that you will need to travel to Upperworld in order to work with your spirit guides, angels, ancestors or even Deities.

SKILLS OF HEDGE RIDING

Some basic skills of hedge riding that you will develop and master over time are protection, divination, astral projection and shapeshifting; these are valuable skills for the hedge witch to possess as you will use more than one of the aforementioned skills during your hedge crossing career.

PROTECTION

When you cross the hedge or hedge ride, you are allowing your spirit to leave your body. As you become more experienced, you will find yourself journeying further away from your physical form, so it is of utmost importance that you protect yourself and not allow harm to come to your body while you are not in it. I would suggest before undergoing any sort of hedge riding or crossing to make sure your protection is in good order.

Protection is really a key component of any magical practice, whether it is crossing the hedge, working magic, circle-casting or simply warding the home in order to protect the occupants and property. One could argue that protection is something that a witch should be doing regularly whether working magic or not; keeping oneself safe in general is always good practice.

There are several different ways to protect yourself while crossing. It is up to the individual witch as to what works best, but here are some suggestions:

Anointing oil: an excellent tool to use when journeying, oils can be loaded with powerful herbs with strong protective qualities. If you are handy with crafting your own oils, you can select the herbs that you find work best for you in protective magic. If not, there is a recipe at the end of the book to help you formulate your own oil for protection.

Talismans: If you have ever watched a horror movie you will no doubt be familiar with the concept of a talisman. Most often the talisman was cursed, connected to a dead person, or offered protection to the person wearing it who would then lose it at a pivotal moment in the plot. But what exactly is a talisman and what does it do?

A talisman is an object, more often than not a small pendant or disc shaped item, that is believed to be imbued with some sort of magical power. A very basic example would be the pentagram that a witch wears; the pentagram is believed to offer protection and represent the five elements. Even the cross that is worn by Christians is a type of talisman, if they believe it connects them to God and offers some sort of protection against evil or temptation.

A talisman would be an important part of your crossing journey; it will offer protection whilst traversing the realms. It is a connection to your spirit and can be your physical connection to your body and sacred space. Talismans can also be anointed and held in the hand when crossing, for a dual tool that protects in this world and the next world. The talisman can be as simple or as elaborate as you like; performing a protection ritual on the item you are using will empower it further with your personal energy. Examples of talismans and suggestions for making one are in Chapter 7.

Sigils: A sigil is a hand-drawn symbol that holds meaning to the person who created it and is empowered toward a specific task or action. Sigils have a long history in magical practice most often associated with chaos magic, angelic beings and, in some schools of thought, the Seals of Solomon. There are a lot of instructional websites and videos that go into sigil magic in great detail. Sigils have no hard or fast rules and generally, as long as the symbol means something to you, it will work.

The Seals of Solomon: a set of 44 symbols related to astrological bodies, the Seals of Solomon come from a medieval grimoire called *The Key of Solomon*. While traditionally associated with ceremonial magic rather than hedge witchery, they can be quite useful across the board for all sorts of magical work. The Fifth Pentacle of the Sun invokes spirits that can help transport you from one place to another; the Sixth Pentacle provides invisibility. One most helpful to the hedge witch would be the Third Pentacle of the Moon, which protects against the danger of travel and will provide protection against attacks, as does the Sixth Pentacle of Mars. So as you can see, while not necessarily a tool in traditional or hedge witchcraft, the seals do offer possibilities for protective and hedge riding magic.

Runes: Runic are perhaps one of the more famous forms of ancient magical symbolism. Modern rune sets are made from relatively small discs or squares that can be tucked into your top whilst journeying, or placed into your hedge bag as one of your tools to take with you and use in Otherworld. *Algiz* is perhaps the best-known protective rune. You could also create a small tablet with several runes to represent the journey in total such as *Eihwaz* for defense, *Teiwaz* or *Tyr* for warrior energy, and *Raido* for journeying. You could even use the *Helm of Awe* as a protective rune, or create a slightly larger disc and wear it as a talisman.

DIVINATION

One element of magical practice, whether hedge crossing or otherwise, is divination. The purpose of hedge crossing on most occasions is to divine the answers to situations or help with works you are performing as a witch. But you can also use various divination methods whilst in a trance state to seek out answers, look for patterns and receive prophetic messages.

In the world of divining, there is a method for everyone. If tarot doesn't suit you, try tea leaf reading or runes. While the different forms of divination could be a book all of their own, let's look at the most common forms that most witches will practice.

Tarot: Tarot is probably one of the most famous divination methods there is. The variety of card decks out there is breathtaking, with something that will suit everyone. Again, this is an art form that could have and has had many books written on it and a little research will bring up some truly fantastic books on the topic.

A tarot deck consists of 78 cards: 22 Major Arcana cards that often address big situations in life, archetypal themes and the soul's journey, and the Minor Arcana, consisting of 56 cards in 4 suits (Wands, Swords, Pentacles and Cups), which tend to address the more mundane or common daily situations in life. Tarot is heavily based on reading the symbols within the cards and applying them to the question or situation being asked about. It has an unfailing honesty for the most part, and I find it can be a little brutally straight forward.

Oracle: Oracle cards are the younger cousin of Tarot, having come into existence in the 1800s with the advent of the Lenormand oracle; the oldest known deck of the Lenormand is kept in the British Museum. The name comes from Marie Anne Lenormand, a well-known cartomancer in the 1800's; her cards were the forerunner of the modern oracle deck.

Oracle cards, like tarot, come in many different sizes and themes. Unlike tarot, which is a more fixed system of divination, oracle decks can vary anywhere from 25 to 56 cards, depending on the author's vision and interpretation of their vision. Oracle cards are quite a bit gentler than tarot, and tend to guide you toward an answer. Oracle card answers also vary depending on the deck's theme; a deck based around vampires is going to give you different answers than a deck based around mermaids.

Runes: Runes are nearly as well-known as tarot as a divination tool. Runic alphabets – created by Odin according to the *Hávamál* - come from Germanic and Scandinavian countries and appear in archeological evidence as early as 150AD. Runes don't generally predict the future but can be used in conjunction with tools that are. Runes are used to more provide guidance and advice.

There is a wide variety of runes for divination out there, made from gemstones to wood to stone and bone. Rune sets generally consist of 24 runes of the Elder Futhark alphabet. As discussed earlier, these symbols have been adopted in modern magical practice to use in inscriptions, such as on protective amulets and talismans, in addition to divination.

Scrying: Most often done with a crystal ball or a bowl filled with water, scrying is another famous divination method used throughout time and often portrayed in movies. A simple black bowl of water will yield fantastic results. One could also use a black mirror. These are actually quite cheap to make: paint a glass insert from a photo frame with black paint, place it back into the frame, and you will have one ready-to-use mirror. Of course if you are artistically inclined, you could decorate the mirror to reflect your beliefs and aesthetic preferences. The same goes for scrying bowls—if you are handy with ceramics or pottery, it would be quite easy to make one that is personal to you and your practice.

Pendulum: A pendulum consists of a long cord with a weighted object on the bottom that will allow it to swing. The way it swings reveals divine answers as guided by the energy or will of the person holding the other end. Pendulum reading can be as simple or as complicated as you like. It can range from a very basic yes/no answer situation to a more detailed sitting using a pendulum board.

The great thing about modern times is that there is a plethora of pendulums available for purchase; from elaborate multicolored stones to simple wood or stone ones. I would suggest selecting a pendulum made out of a medium that resonates with you; if you've always felt drawn to amethyst then you will likely work quite well with an amethyst pendulum.

If you wish to delve deeper into working with a pendulum, a pendulum board will help expand and enhance answers. A board consists of sections for the pendulum to swing to in order to give you the answers you seek. Some are quite elaborate, reminiscent of the layout of a Ouija board; others will simply have Yes/No/Don't Know as the available answers.

Tea Leaf Reading: Tasseomancy, or the art of reading tea leaves, is another traditional, old-school form of divination. A tasseomancer will usually have you think on what you would like guidance or answers for, then drink your loose leaf tea, swishing it about a bit. When you finish, the leaves at the bottom will reveal symbols and shapes that guide the reading. It can be a bit of a harder method to learn because there are so many different symbols and signs that can be revealed, but a good book on tea leaf reading can help with a basic understanding of what the shapes mean.

As you further learn and grow; it is possible to intuitively interpret the signs in the cup. Let the leaves speak to you and give impressions of what they mean based on what you feel looking at them. This is definitely a more intuitive and empathic approach, so I would suggest having a basic grounding in the commonly shared meanings first.

Mediumship: Mediumship is the ability to speak with the Dead. As a hedge witch, it is entirely possible that you will find yourself also being a psychopomp (one who guides souls to the other side) or a conduit for the Dead to impart messages and speak with their loved ones. Mediumship is a form of divination that gained widespread notoriety during the early 1900's, as it was something of an entertainment. While there were some serious practitioners who could speak with the Dead, there were those who were not above performing tricks to unsuspecting clientele.

Mediums may use any of the above-mentioned divination methods, as well as channeling, Ouija, automatic writing, trance and séances to contact the Dead. As with any working or practice where you are dealing with spirits or beings that are not of this world, it is recommended that you always have protections in place in order to prevent them from harming you or disrupting your life in any way.

Ogham: Ogham (also referred to as ogham Staves and Celtic ogham) are small sticks of wood carved with symbols from the Celtic ogham alphabet. There are twenty letters in the ogham alphabet, each representing a sound as well as a tree. There are still stones with ogham carved on them in Ireland and other parts of the Celtic world. For divination purposes, the meaning of each letter is associated with the energies of the tree it is named for. For example, Birch (Beith) is the letter B, and is indicative of new beginnings, new growth and generally positive things. Yew (Ioho) represents the letter I, and is indicative of protection, renewal and ancestor work.

A traditional ogham stave set would have 20 different woods, with each letter being made from the wood of the tree it represents. But if ogham is a divination tool that speaks to you, it's not necessary to have each type of wood—you can use one kind of wood to carve the symbols into, or purchase one of the many lovely sets available online.

Throwing Bones: Throwing the bones, or cleromancy, is another ancient divination method found in cultures from Africa to Asia. It is also a very interesting and complex form, as no two sets of throwing bones are the same, and no two sets hold the same meanings. Foundational sets are often for sale online but most readers will build and create their own. The sets may consist only of animal bones, but often also include other small objects such as:

- Gemstones
- Plants and Roots
- Shells
- Seeds
- Teeth
- Runes
- Dice
- Charms
- Marbles
- Pendants
- Buttons

Generally when it comes to throwing bones, the meanings will be something the diviner personally attributes to each piece. To read the bones, one focuses on the question and then quite literally throws them—not an overhead throw of course, but a gentle throw onto a mat or cloth that will have designated areas with meanings in order to read. Each cloth will also differ from reader to reader. There is no one way or right way to read the bones—this is a highly personal divinatory tool that speaks directly to the reader's own intuition and interpretations.

ASTRAL PROJECTIONS

Astral projection is the layman's term used to describe an out of body experience (OBE) induced by trance, meditation, visualization or self-hypnosis. It has a long and storied history as a tool to explore Otherworld and/or other realms. It is often described as a thread connecting your body to your soul that is seen to be leaving the physical form and journeying to the astral realm or plane. thereby allowing the projector to meet with other people, travel to other places and perform tasks that they may not be able to do in their physical body.

Astral projection is a term that often brings about derision and disbelief but is possible to do with practice. Children often find themselves able to astral project without too many issues; I believe this is because children are more malleable and open, not having had the world teach them differently yet. I used to astral project as a child; this is where I first met my guide. I am not as successful at it as I once was, I lost the ability once I hit puberty and other things became a distraction. Having to relearn it has required quite a bit of dedication.

Astral projection and hedge riding are not dissimilar in nature. Hedge riding or crossing allows you to leave your body and travel to other planes and other realms; it gives you the freedom to move as you wish and perform workings, gather information, meet with other souls and work with your guides. Many hedge witches make a distinction between the two, since hedge riding takes place within Otherworld, made up of the three worlds, which is defined differently than the astral plane. But others don't observe this distinction and use the terms interchangeably.

Once you learn to hedge cross or astral project, the world and many other worlds are your oyster. Astral projection is a deep subject and too vast to share within the confines of this book, but I would definitely recommend researching and investigating guided meditations to get you started. Your local library may have some great resources, and there are many online videos and meditations to help you as well.

SHAPESHIFTING

If there is one thing that speaks to the soul of a hedge witch it is shapeshifting: the ability to turn oneself into an animal and leap through the spiritual realms with freedom and without a care. There is nothing more liberating than allowing your primal soul to journey, to shift and shape into a beast, embracing the traits and abilities of said beast. This is where your animal guide or fetch beast will be the most helpful.

Often, a witch will shift herself into the shape of her fetch or guide and traverse Otherworld as that form. However you can change yourself into whatever animal, bird or reptile suits you best. If you feel as though the journey will be more beneficial in the form of a leopard, then go for it; often the keen senses and reflexes of big cats can be very helpful. However, the stoicism and stealth of a wolf will keep you in the shadows until you are ready to reveal yourself. Or you could change yourself into a hare as Isobel Gowdie, the famous witch from Auldearn, Scotland, did.

She shared during her trial and confessions her charm for changing into a hare and back again:

To take the likeness of a hare:

> *I shall go into a hare,*
> *With sorrow and sych and meickle care;*
> *And I shall go in the Devil's name,*
> *Ay while I come home again.*

To shift back:

> *Hare, hare, God send thee care.*
> *I am in a hare's likeness now,*
> *But I shall be in a woman's likeness even now.*

—Robert Pitcairn, *Ancient Criminal Trials in Scotland* (1833)

Shapeshifting has such a rich history throughout the world, from werewolves to skinwalkers to witches changing shape into their chosen spirit form, to bats becoming vampires, to Gods such as Proteus and Loki. There is diverse lore the world over about shapeshifters who would shift into other forms in order to enact their desires, magic, trickery, escape or to live.

To change into an animal is not easy; it requires a lot of concentration and work in order to successfully pull it off without depleting your energy. To shapeshift successfully you have to know the animal you are changing into. Of course it is understood that having had physical contact with the animal is not necessary; I'd not recommend you try and make friends with a bear in the wild in order to figure out how to shapeshift into one.

Watch the animal... Use videos online, or if you are lucky

enough to be able to safely watch one in its natural habitat, then do so. Watch how it moves, how it eats, and listen to its vocalizing. See how it interacts with others of its kind, and how it acts by itself. Begin to feel the energy of the animal within yourself. Feel your limbs become its limbs, feel your eyesight become its eyesight, move slowly and deliberately, feeling every bit of the animal.

In order to shapeshift successfully, you have to believe you will. You have to be able to realistically feel as though you are changing into the animal. It's not something that can be done easily and in one session. The art of shapeshifting will take some time but your guides will often help you with it and show you the way. This is why I suggest first learning to shapeshift into your animal guide; you will have its support and guidance, and you will find more success. Once you have mastered changing into your animal guide's form, you will find adapting the process to change into other animals much easier.

Chapter Four:
METHODS OF TRANCE

An important step to learning to cross the hedge is being able to induce a trance state in order to shift your conscious mind into being receptive to journeying. What is a trance exactly? The Oxford dictionary defines it as "a half-conscious state characterized by an absence of response to external stimuli, typically as induced by hypnosis or entered by a medium."

A trance state allows the conscious mind to open and receive experiences and visions that come from the subconscious mind. Shamans, healers and mystics the world over in history would go into trance states to converse with spirits, seek knowledge and hear messages.

Perhaps the best example of going into a trance state is the Oracle of Delphi. The Oracle would inhale a suffumigation and enter a trance state; from that she would announce visions and prophecy that would be interpreted and shared with the ruler of the time.

There is much debate about what exactly caused the Oracle to enter the trance state. Some historical lore suggests it was henbane (*Hyoscyamus niger*) or another herb with similar psychotropic qualities; however, some archeological evidence has shown that the source of the fumes the Oracle inhaled may have been ethylene or a mix of carbon dioxide and methane coming up through a fissure in the oracle room. Whatever it was, the Oracle at Delphi illustrates the long history of using external stimuli to induce a trance state for the purposes of mystical or magical experiences.

In our own times, the use of chemical psychedelics like LSD, DMT, or MDMA, and natural substances such as peyote, cannabis, ayahuasca, psilocybin and solanaceae plants show that the fascination with trance states and the possibility of wisdom or knowledge obtained from them are very attractive in this fast-paced world. However, many of the above-mentioned examples are illegal or highly unadvisable without experience, and there are several other ways that a person can enter a trance state without chemical help.

Any of the methods described here will assist in achieving a trance or altered state. Some will work for you; others perhaps not so much. Being able to get into a trance state is dependent on how receptive you are to stimuli, how easily you can focus, and how easily you are able to let go of your conscious mind. Believe it or not, this last one is the hardest because it means giving up an element of control, which is not something most of us are used to doing. Trance or altered states are entirely achievable with practice and determination; once you learn how to achieve a trance state, you will find hedge crossing very easy to do.

DRUMMING

Drumming offers a consistent rhythmic beat that can lull the mind into a trance state. When you are drumming to enter trance, your mind is focused on the task at hand. You will find yourself blocking out any external distractions as your mind zeroes in on the beat, concentrating on making sure the rhythm is stable and continual before slowly building into a faster beat. This singular focus or concentration is the key to achieving trance.

Several years ago I was involved in a ritual for the Autumn Equinox; we were in a circular tower room with drums all around the balcony. As they were played it fed into the heartbeat of the practitioners below and moved us in really amazing ways. Afterwards, everyone felt as though had we moved into another realm—such was the power of the beat while working magic.

CHANTING

You are most likely already familiar with the idea of chanting, whether you do it in spells, to seal work, or simply as an exercise to focus the mind. Much like drumming, chanting allows our brains to focus on one task and block out external distractions. Chanting is as simple as the *Om* chant in yoga or as lengthy as the Gregorian chants sung in religious orders.

Within the Wiccan tradition there is the chant of the Goddess' names ("Isis, Astarte, Diana, Hecate, Demeter, Kali, Inanna"), which, when said consistently and repetitively, will shift the perception of the mind. All kinds of chants can facilitate a change in perception, and can induce a trance state when used in a focused, intentional way.

BREATHWORK

If you practice regular meditation or yoga, you will be familiar with the idea of breathwork. During meditation, one will often use breath as a way to focus the mind away from distracting thoughts. In yoga, breath is used as you move through the positions in order to induce a state of oneness and connectedness with the mind and body. It is used to relax you, to allow for ease of movement, and to block out external issues and direct thoughts inward.

Breathwork is a valuable tool to learn and while some argue it can't bring about a trance state on its own, it does often help calm the mind, shift perception, and relax the body, which can only assist in achieving an altered state.

ECSTATIC DANCE

From the Maenads and Korybantes of Greek lore to the traditional dances in Haitian Vodou, dance has been used for millennia to bring about an altered state. Ecstatic dance allows you to completely free your mind from your physical conscious self and allow the energy of the music to move you in a purely primal way.

Dance is a powerful expression of who we are and of our spirit; it is an opportunity to drop our ego, leaving us to just feel and be very present in the moment. Ritual dance, contemporary dance, and even dancing in a club shows how music and movement can induce an altered state and take us to other places without us even realizing it. Ecstatic dance can be performed by itself or used in conjunction with other trance aids, allowing for a fully immersive experience.

MUSIC

Music is something that moves us all. Every time a song comes on that we know, we are moved through the timeline of our minds to memories associated with that song. While that's not exactly a trance state specifically, it does illustrate the ability for music to transport our minds somewhere else.

There are some fantastic pagan musicians out there creating gorgeous music with chants, drums and lyrics that can aid in attaining an altered state. One of my most favorite songs for this is "The Mystic's Dream" by Loreena McKennit. It has drums, chants, string instruments and a beautiful lyrical beat; when this song plays, you can't help but move with it.

MEDITATION AND VISUALIZATION

One of the foundational skills of spell working is meditation and visualization. This is one of the first things you learn when foraying into the mystical arts; without these skills, your spell and ritual work generally doesn't have much punch behind it. In most cases, in order to push energy toward the results of your workings, you will typically visualize the end result. See the spell coming to fruition, see the ritual working, and imagine the outcome.

While hedge crossing is not visualization or meditation, it does involve elements of these processes, and it is good practice to be able to meditate and visualize in order to enhance the skills you do need to hedge cross. Visualization allows you to hold the image of Otherworld in your mind while you cross; meditation allows you to quiet your mind so it can be receptive to entering an altered state. When combining these two elements, you have the beginnings of being able to journey.

Chapter Five: THE HEDGE WITCH'S HERBAL

Herbs have been powerful allies to witches the world over. Depending on location, a witch could find a wealth of options in their neck of the woods and know how to use them magically and mundanely to make the most of what she had. A hedge witch who is worth their weight will know how to use herbs to craft potent magic, including healing brews, herbal charms, baths, incenses, ointments and more.

Herbs are an endless and bountiful magical tool. They hold the lifeblood of the earth in their DNA; the energy is from the Universe itself. Each herb, tree, and flower has its own unique set of correspondences, its own unique purpose. During spellwork and ritual the herbs provide energy that can be tapped into, infusing poppets, charms, amulets and a multitude of other items to help focus power and bring about the desired change.

From the wild herbs that grow in forests and on the road's edge, to the herbs and trees that grow plentifully in the hedgerows or in your own garden, there is nothing quite like working with herbs to give your rituals and spells a big boost.

HERBS OF THE HEDGE

As mentioned earlier, in the past the word "hedge" signified both the physical hedge that separated a community from the wilder countryside, and the spiritual hedge that hedge witches would use in order to "cross the veil" or "straddle the hedge" in order to perform their spiritual works. The herbs found within hedgerows could offer very powerful medicine, for both spiritual and physical healing. Here, we will look at some common herbs that could be found in a hedgerow, along with a few of their traditional magical and medicinal applications.

CAUTION: *When using herbs in a medicinal fashion, always consult your physician or clinical herbalist. Herbs can interact with medications, or be contraindicated for various conditions. Without proper guidance or knowledge it would be too easy to harm yourself through incorrect use or dosage.*

Blackberry (Bramble)
(*Rubus fruiticosus*)

The blackberry (or bramble) has a long and well-known history both magically and mundanely. It is one of those plants that are both bane and beauty of the plant world. It makes delicious jam and medicinal tea, and attracts beneficial bugs to your garden (and goats are known to decimate it in fairly quick fashion). However this very helpful plant is also an invasive one that can take over a space in little to no time, branching out everywhere and shooting up runners. Yet it has been invaluable as a hedge plant. Blackberry can either be thornless or have thorns; the thornless variety is a cultivar that was created to make it easier for home gardeners. The blackberry you would often find in the hedgerow would most definitely have had thorns.

Medicinally, blackberry has often been used to treat pain, swelling, gout, diarrhea and fluid retention. It can also be used to help soothe irritation in the throat and mouth. This effect is said to come from its high content of tannins and Vitamin C. Magically speaking, the blackberry is first and foremost protective; the thorns will rip and tear at you if you try and get through them. This makes blackberry a beneficial addition to any protective magic. Blackberry also makes a great representation on the altar as a physical piece of the metaphysical hedge. The leaves are great for healing and wealth works. Traditionally, blackberries were baked into pies to celebrate Lughnasadh, the Celtic harvest festival.

Crab Apple
(*Malus sylvestris*)

With its delicate pink and white flowers and small fruits, the crab apple is a delightful bush to look at. It is an excellent pollinator in an apple orchard, and it's also incredibly helpful food-wise – I'm sure a lot of people have grandmothers who have crab apple jam or jelly recipes.

Apples of all kinds have a long history of magical uses, so the crab apple—the original wild apple—also packs a magical punch.

The Celts believed that apples had the power of healing, youth, rebirth and love. However, apples can be found in magical lore from many different cultures and religions around the world—from the story of Adam and Eve to the Poetic Eddas of the Norse. A crab apple tree would have provided food, healing and magical tools for the hedge witch, from charms and wands to cider, juice, jams and stews, and as such would have been a very versatile magical ally.

Dandelion
(*Taraxacum officinalis*)

A plant used for luck, spirit work, and wishes, dandelion is an absolute powerhouse both medicinally and magically. It's also important nutritionally, as the leaves of the dandelion can be eaten cooked or raw (sautéed with some garlic and butter is always delicious) and are an excellent source of vitamins A, C, K, E, and a little bit of B. They also contain folate, iron, calcium, magnesium and potassium. Dandelion root is a great coffee substitute and when roasted has a rich, dark flavor. For our ancestors, dandelion would have served as a good food source, as the whole plant can be used.

Dandelion tea is a good tool for promoting psychic powers and leaving as an offering for spirits. (However, dandelion is a diuretic, so please do not over-consume.) The flowers would make an exceptionally good offering to place on your altar to the spirits and Guardians of the Otherworlds, as dandelion is a humble plant yet has a lot of strength within it. It can survive some serious attacks from over-enthusiastic lawn lovers in a bid to keep their lawns pristine, and it will always return and thrive.

Marshmallow
(*Althea officinalis*)

A beautiful and stately flower that grows wild, althea, or marshmallow, is a powerful spirit herb and an equally powerful healer. The root is a mucilaginous herb, meaning that when steeped it creates something of a gooey consistency. (Side fact: althea root was used to make marshmallows long before the sugary confection we know today came about.) Given its mucilaginous properties, marshmallow is often used to soothe sore throats and dry coughs, as it coats the throat and provides moisture and protection for mucus membranes.

Marshmallow root is also a strong spirit herb. An incense of marshmallow burned with other complimentary spirit herbs such as myrrh or copal will attract spirits of a kinder or more helpful nature. A small vial or jar of it on your ancestor altar would help in bringing them to your sacred space and aid in communication. The "fluff" (as I call it) from ground marshmallow root is an excellent stuffing for poppets and dolls to use in magical work—it would be especially good in healing works or works to attract a particular spirit into the poppet or doll.

Raspberry
(*Rubus idaeus*)

The humble raspberry with its tart red fruit and fluffy leaves is a staple in the orchard, but it's also a plant that grows within the wild hedgerow. The raspberry is quite common in the supermarket now, and while the fruit is rather delicious and would have been a great edible for our forebears, it is the plant itself that offers the most value.

Raspberry, despite its common appearance, is a protective herb. Cultivars today are thornless, to make it easier for home gardeners to work with, but in the wild the plants do have thorns. Thorns are an especially potent symbol of protection; and the branches of the raspberry can be fashioned into a protective amulet or talisman to be hung up in doors and windows. The raspberry is also a plant of love; it has long been used to promote fidelity, fertility and romantic love. It is said that this herb can bring luck in matters of marriage, motherhood and attraction.

Raspberry is also an astringent and stimulant, giving it the ability to strengthen and tone pelvic muscles. Pregnant women will often drink raspberry leaf tea to help stimulate the uterus in the later stages of labour to help ease the birth. However, there is disagreement about whether raspberry leaves are safe during early pregnancy, so if you are pregnant, please do not ingest nor soak in this plant unless under the supervision of a herbalist or medical practitioner. Aside from helping with birth; raspberry leaf also helps with sore throats and PMS. It can promote healing by helping tighten up the skin around wounds, and can offer a cooling effect on the body to help reduce heat and inflammation.

Rosehip
(*Rosa rubiginosa/canina*)

Rosehip is one of the most abundant and sturdy herbs to grow in the wild. In my area there are quite a lot growing wild on the side of the road, yet these plants are surprisingly difficult to propagate from cuttings or grow from seed. (But such is the nature of plants in the *Rosa* family.) Rosehip is very high in vitamin C, vitamin A, and various antioxidants, making it a nice little powerhouse when used in teas, jams, pies, and other foods and beverages. I wouldn't suggest you pick a ripe rosehip and eat it, however, because it is lined with fluffy little hairs that will make you feel as though you've swallowed a bottle of itching powder. Rosehip is also fantastic for the skin and hair, promoting growth, lusciousness, and overall health.

Rosehip is a thorny hedge plant that offers wonderful protective powers, but also is good for calling in spirits – especially in matters of love. It is said that rosehip can help heal a broken heart and restore faith in the emotion of love, in addition to encouraging love to come to you. A dried branch or small bottle of rosehip next to the bed will help ensure the protection of the mind during sleep, keeping it free from nightmares and the intrusion of darker spirits. Using a small vial of rosehip while crossing the hedge—perhaps in an amulet around your neck—would certainly offer those protective powers as you journey.

Stinging Nettle
(*Urtica dioica*)

Although the nettle has been much maligned, it is a hugely helpful and industrious worker. It has a long history of being used as medicine, food, rope and fiber. It's an excellent tonic for the hair, helping control dandruff and adding shine. An old remedy for conditioning the hair is nettle leaf steeped in apple cider vinegar and used as a rinse. It's also incredibly nourishing with plenty of vitamin A and C, along with iron, potassium, manganese, and calcium, and even a fair bit of protein. In fact, it is said that nettle is better for you than spinach. If you're a lover of the brew, nettle beer could be for you as it was once a favorite in rural Britain.

Nettle is also a powerfully protective herb, known to break jinxes and curses, assist in uncrossing people, and protect animals and people from supernatural attacks. Lore says that nettle can also ward off lightning strikes, so it would be a good herb to hang up around the home to protect the perimeter and those within. Dried nettle can be used as a stuffing for a poppet, or you could even create your own "nettle dolly" (in the same fashion as a corn dolly) to use in sympathetic magic.

(Of course, given its name, I would caution against harvesting nettle barehanded as it can give quite the nasty sting).

Saint John's Wort
(*Hypericum perforatum*)

Saint (or St.) John's wort, named for John the Baptist, is one of my most favorite herbs; I don't think any witch's cabinet is complete without it. It has such a spirit about it that you can't help but love working with it. When infused in oil, it turns the most glorious red color. Medicinally, St. John's wort packs a punch as a healer, anti-depressant and pain reliever. It works to help with moderate depression and seasonal affective disorder, and has been shown to help with anxiety. Externally, it's used to treat mild burns, cuts, abrasions, and bruises. It can also be effective in helping relieve tired and sore muscles when applied topically as a liniment, oil or ointment. Note: This is an herb that should not be used internally unless under the supervision of a doctor or herbalist, as St John's wort does contraindicate with quite a lot of different medications.

St John's wort is fantastic for keeping unwanted spirits out of the house. A *saining* (or blessing and protection) spray could be made with this herb, accompanied by other cleansing/exorcising herbs and salted water in a spray bottle. Spray it around your sacred space while reciting your preferred prose or verses to rid the house of unwanted company. This herb is also known for its love divination qualities—a sprig under the pillow will help reveal your future spouse in dreams. It is traditionally harvested on Friday, the day of love, as well as at Midsummer, when its bountiful and bright yellow flowers show its connection to Solar magic.

Valerian
(*Valeriana officinalis*)

It might wrinkle the nose with its wet and musty odor of old socks, but valerian is one of the most well-known healing herbs, used the world over as a remedy for insomnia and sleep disorders. In fact, if you go to any health aisle of the supermarket you will see numerous remedies for sleep with valerian in them. Its history of healing and helping with insomnia and restlessness can be found back into antiquity, with Hippocrates himself extolling the virtues of valerian.

I've always equated valerian as something of a *chthonic* (or "Underworld") herb. I prefer to use it in works with Ancestors and dreaming, opening oneself up to communication and information provided from the other side. It is also quite protective and would often be used to guard against lightning strikes and ill intentions. Given valerian's earthy tones and aroma, it is also quite a good herb to use when working animal magic. Incidentally, much like catnip, cats adore valerian root, but as with catnip, it's hit-or-miss as to whether your cat will enjoy the scent or be indifferent.

Yarrow
(*Achillea millefolium*)

If there ever was an MVP of the herbal world it would be yarrow; it is a power player both medicinally and magically and can offer so much to us. Yarrow is associated with the legend of Achilles. It is said that the herb sprouted from the rust shaved from his spear and that he used the herb to treat the wounds of his soldiers, which is not surprising as yarrow is quite the impactful healer. Yarrow is a *styptic*, an herb that when powdered can help reduce blood flow from a wound. It is antibacterial, anti-inflammatory, reduces fever, and can clear sinuses, as well as being good for healing bruises, wounds and deep cuts. An ointment of yarrow (coupled with another super healer like comfrey) would make a fantastic all-around healing balm.

Magically speaking, yarrow is a powerful protector and should always be included in balms, brews or bags that are used in conjunction with astral projection, hedge crossing and other spirit work. (I will use hedge riding and hedge crossing interchangeably in this book simply because they are more or less the same thing.) A tea of yarrow will help open the mind to those around us who wish to communicate, or to open the psychic channels and allow messages to come through. It will enhance dreams and allow prophetic dreams to float to the surface whilst keeping us safe from things that might try to cross over or latch on. It is said that yarrow sprinkled across the doorway will prevent negative spirits from crossing the threshold and wreaking havoc in the home. Yarrow is really pretty to grow as well, coming in a multitude of colors.

Be warned—it shoots from runners, so if you plant it in your garden, it will take over. So be prepared to be forever harvesting yarrow if it is grown uncontained (although having an abundance of yarrow is not necessarily a bad thing).

HERBS OF THE HEDGE WITCH – THE BANES

"Oh, I have been beyond the town, Where nightshade black and mandrake grow, and I have been and I have seen What righteous folk would fear to know!"

—Doreen Valiente, "The Witch's Ballad" (1978)

This hedge witch's herbal wouldn't be complete if we didn't look at some of the more famous herbs used by witches throughout history to create flying ointments to help slip the skin and cross the hedge. This section is by no means an endorsement to try any of the herbs described here—they require an experienced hand and the guidance of someone very knowledgeable in the application and use of baneful herbs.

Baneful herbs are named so because of their nature—they are poisonous and deadly, known throughout history for their hallucinogenic properties. They were herbs not lightly used but often abused, especially by those who did not understand or know the spirit of the plants and what they were capable of.

These were herbs of such power and spirit that the ordinary folk would shudder at the mention of their names, herbs that could poison or heal, depending on how they were used, and herbs that would allow the witch to fly from her body and journey the length and breadth of the Universe. These are the herbs known throughout history as herbs of witches, and have been thought to grow in every witch's garden.

The information offered here is deliberately sparse in terms of usage, simply because without proper guidance or experience, there can be extremely harmful and serious consequences from using these baneful herbs. Traveling with the spirit of any of the plants described here could spell disaster or death for the unwary, untrained or unknowing.

There is a legend that tells of a brigade of English soldiers out of Jamestown in Virginia who mistook *Datura stramonium* for edible greens and spent 11 days experiencing some truly powerful hallucinations. Some thought they were monkeys; others simply sat in their own excrement and drooled. Without proper experience, guidance and knowledge, the herbs contained in the Banes part of this chapter will teach you harsh lessons that will affect you for the rest of your life.

It is simply not enough to read about the herb and consider yourself ready. You must get to know the plant, its quirks, its personality and most of all, its deadly nature. Start with Mugwort or Wormwood; learn the energy of each before you consider moving on to their stronger compatriots. The foremost lesson of the Banes is to never forget to respect the plant; for its nature is powerful, wild and dark, and capable of incredible and devastating acts.

CAUTION: *The following descriptions are for informational purposes only, I highly recommend that you do not work with, grow or touch any of these plants unless you are experienced in working with herbs of a toxic and deadly nature and know what you are doing. If you work with these herbs without the necessary training or knowledge, you risk poisoning, grievous injury and death.*

Aconite
(*Aconitum napellus*)

Aconite, also known as monkshood or wolfsbane, is an herb known both for its stunningly beautiful purple flowers and its deadly toxicity. Native to Europe and Asia, aconite is a hardy perennial that loves the shade and can grow up to five feet tall, but is highly dangerous to humans and animals. Plants of the aconite family were often rumored to cure lycanthropy, and offer invisibility and protection from vampires and werewolves.

In *Harry Potter and the Prisoner of Azkaban*, Professor Lupin drinks a potion of wolfsbane to help prevent his transformation into a werewolf. This detail may have been inspired by a practice of ancient Greek shepherds, who used bait laced with aconite to kill wolves who endangered their flocks.

Black Hellebore
(*Helleborus niger*)

Black hellebore is part of the *Ranunculacae* family (the same family as the buttercup). Also known as the Christmas rose, winter rose, or snow rose, this evergreen plant produces gorgeous black flowers during winter. They are quite hardy, which makes them very popular in hard-to-grow places in the garden, as well as in cottage gardens. However, they are toxic.

Black hellebore was rumored to cure madness, and was used to assist in exorcism and banishing. It was also often thought to be a plant witches used to summon demons. In Greek mythology, black hellebore is the plant that was used to save the daughters of King Argos, who were sent mad by the god Dionysus.

Black Nightshade
(*Solanum nigrum*)

Black nightshade is the lesser toxic cousin of belladonna (deadly nightshade). The green berries are toxic, but the black ripe ones are often cooked and eaten in some tribal regions. However, this is something I would not recommend trying unless you're quite familiar with the plant.

Black nightshade is often confused with its deadlier cousin because the two plants do look very similar, but black nightshade berries grow in bunches, whereas deadly nightshade grows in individual berries. This plant has lovely white or purple flowers and grows roughly one to two feet in height. It is an annual, and once it has taken up residence in your garden, it tends to grow and offshoot everywhere.

Datura
(*Datura inoxia/stramonium/metel*)

Datura, also known as jimson weed, is one of the more deadly of the witches' herbs and has interesting folklore names like devil's apple and thorn apple. It is highly toxic and must be handled very carefully should you find this in your garden.

It grows to about two feet high and is said to have a strange odor. Datura can be used to break hexes, manipulative spells, or any other spells cast against you. It is a particularly dangerous plant to ingest and can cause very severe hallucinations, poisoning, and long-term physical issues.

Deadly Nightshade/Belladonna
(*Atropa belladonna*)

This plant is one of legend and lore. There has probably never been a tale about a witch told without mentioning the infamous belladonna, one of the many herbs in medieval flying ointments. It is often called the witch's berry, bane wort, or fair lady, and has also been referred to as Hecate's mandrake. Both mandrake and belladonna come from the *Solanaceae* family, interestingly the same family as the potato, tomato, tobacco and eggplant.

Long before it was made famous as a witch's plant, belladonna was used as an anesthetic. However, the same toxic alkaloids in belladonna that made it a useful anesthetic also cause hallucinations and death, and can seriously damage a person's health if used incorrectly. In antiquity, it was also used by women to dilate the pupils to appear more beautiful. To illustrate how deadly this plant is, its Latin name references Atropos from the three Fates of Greek mythology—the one who cuts the threads of life.

Common Foxglove
(*Digitalis purpurea*)

Foxglove is a very popular and lovely cottage garden plant; it holds the chemical compound that makes up the heart medication *Digitalis*. Foxglove is highly toxic and should always be handled with care. A biennial plant, foxglove blooms in late spring and can grow up to 3ft in height.

Foxglove is a very popular faery flower; some of the folklore names for it are fairy's glove and fairy's weed. It is also called witches' gloves and witches' thimbles. Magically, foxglove can be used for faery spells, deflecting negative magic and protection.

Fly Agaric
(*Amanita muscaria*)

The common names for this plant are death cap, redcap mushroom and raven's bread. It is one of the infamous hallucinatory shrooms that need to be carefully handled if discovered in the wild. It is believed that fly agaric is the world's oldest hallucinogen, used in Lapland and Siberia by Shamans in healing rituals and vision quests.

This mushroom grows in heavily wooded areas in Northern America and Europe. It is the image of the quintessential toadstool and is a motif used often on cards and postcards. Fly agaric is associated with Odin, a shamanic god, and according to folklore can open doorways to the realm of Faery.

Hemlock
(*Conium maculatum*)

Hemlock is definitely another famous witch's herb. It is also known as warlock's weed, poison hemlock and winter fern. Hemlock was once the go-to plant for death by poisoning in ancient Greece, and the classical philosopher Socrates was poisoned by this plant.

Hemlock looks remarkably similar to Queen Anne's lace and wild carrot, so identification is a must with this plant.

Henbane
(*Hyosycamus niger*)

During ancient times, henbane was a popular pain reliever, though it is poisonous in higher doses. Dioscorides recommended it for allaying pains and inducing sleep. Henbane is well known for its use in flying potions. When the Dead used to wander the river Styx, they would wear a crown of henbane. It is thought to have been used in ancient Greece by the oracles to induce trance and visions by inhaling the smoke.

It is a pretty plant with lovely flowers; however, it has been said to smell very unpleasant.

Mandrake
(*Mandragora officinarum*)

Mandrake has to be the most famous plant in magical lore, known throughout the world for many centuries. Once known as the herb of Circe, it was the herb Medea used to help Jason steal the Golden Fleece. It is the root that screamed when it was taken from the pot in *Harry Potter and the Chamber of Secrets*, used to de-petrify the students; it was also used in *Pan's Labyrinth* to try to help Ofelia's mother heal.

Old European legend has it that mandrake grew under the gallows where men hung and their semen dripped creating an alraune, a root shaped in the form of a human housing a familiar spirit. Because of this, building a relationship with the mandrake can be a powerful and prosperous relationship for a witch, as long as the power of the root is respected.

Mugwort
(*Artemisia vulgaris*)

A definite classic of the witch's herbarium, mugwort has been associated with divination, prophecy, astral projection and dreams. An infusion can be used to anoint crystal balls, runes and other divinatory items. Like its cousin wormwood, mugwort is an herbaceous perennial, growing around 1 – 2m tall. Mugwort is sacred to the Druids, and to Diana/Artemis for whom it was named. Stuffed in a pillow, it will bring on prophetic dreams, and drinking an infusion will smooth the way for astral projection.

Mugwort was often used to flavor beer before the introduction of hops; sixty years or so ago it was used in Cornwall as a substitute for tea, as tea was quite expensive. Mugwort is a gentle herb compared to the other, much more overpowering herbs in the baneful category. However, mugwort is an emmenagogue and stimulates the uterus, making it very unsuitable for use by pregnant women, for women who are trying to get pregnant, or women who do not wish to potentially bring on a menstrual cycle.

Wormwood

(*Artemisia absinthium*)

Wormwood is an herbaceous perennial with lovely silver green leaves. It is in the same family as mugwort. It grows to about 3 feet in height and can be grown as a hedge if you desire. The flowers on the wormwood are a lovely sunny yellow color, although not particularly large. Wormwood will bloom late spring/midsummer, depending on the geographic location.

It has a bitter taste and was used to flavor vermouth and absinthe (the famous Green Fairy drink of European origin). It's a popular herb for outdoor work, especially in a cemetery as it is used for summoning spirits and increasing psychic ability. Wormwood is somewhat toxic, so should never be burned inside unless the area is well ventilated.

HARVESTING, DRYING, AND STORING HERBS

A great way to connect with plants is to work with them in both their dried and fresh forms. Dried herbs, when stored correctly, can last quite a long time and add a different layer to your magical work; especially when you have grown them yourself.

A small caveat: While it is amazing to be able to go out into the wild and collect herbs, in some places there has been a thorough stripping and over-harvesting of herbs. Whenever you take from the herbs, take only what you need, never more than that. This way you allow for the herbs to regrow and spread, so the next time you want to harvest there will be an abundance for you to harvest from.

The herbs mentioned in this book are quite common, but as you grow in your practice you will come across other herbs that may be on an endangered or critical list. Always make sure you know the laws surrounding particular herbs. For example, in America, goldenseal (*Hydrastis canadensis*) is considered critically endangered due to over-harvesting and requires a permit to harvest. If you are caught wildcrafting it without a permit, there can be heavy penalties attached.

HARVESTING

There are several different ways to harvest herbs. If you need a root, you will usually harvest the entire plant, taking the root and hopefully finding a use for the leafy material as well. Roots will need a decent wash to get rid of any attached dirt and microbes – you don't want that going into your dried material, especially if you are going to use it in a tea or tincture.

Leaves can be harvested individually or as stems. Flowers are much the same – the entire branch or just the flower head. Seed heads can be picked once the plant has completed its cycle, but you will definitely want to have a bag or sack handy to place the seed head in so that you don't lose them. Some plants like mugwort and nettle have exceptionally fine seeds that can be very hard to see. I would suggest placing your bag over the top of the seed head, pulling it tight around the base, and then snipping, to minimize seed loss.

Plant material is best harvested during the morning, after the dew has dried but before it gets too hot. Really hot sun can bake out the essential oils in the plant so it is important to grab them at the right time of day. However if you are simply using the herbs in a magical way, you can harvest them throughout the day as it suits you. It is important to take precautions when harvesting potentially toxic herbs such as belladonna, or herbs with stingers or thorns. Blackthorn thorns can break off under the skin and cause swelling and pain, and can even turn septic, so it is imperative that you take care when harvesting herbs.

DRYING

There are several different ways to dry herbs once you have harvested them. Some people simply lay them out on trays to dry, but unless you keep them somewhere very dry, this can cause them to molder. The following are some of the more popular and effective ways of drying herbs and roots.

Dehydrator / Oven: Roots and fleshy herbs do well either in a dehydrator or on a low temp in the oven. An oven takes very minimal time when doing leaves and flower petals, meaning you can use your dried herbs a lot quicker than if you let them dry naturally.

You could also use a dehydrator to dry out any fruits or berries that you have harvested by laying them out single layer in the trays and allowing them to dry over a few days. You could also do roots and berries in the oven, though it can be a bit harder to regulate the temperature so that you don't bake or burn them. I like turning it on the absolute lowest heat setting possible and turning the fan on. This circulates the air more evenly and dries the plant material a lot quicker.

Paper Bag: A paper bag is one of the simplest methods of drying herbs. However, you do have to be careful about how much plant material you place in the bag because it can go moldy instead of drying. The good thing about paper bags is that you can peg them up on a line to allow for the warmth of a room to add to drying; or simply store them in a box. Just remember to label them and check them regularly. If there's any sign that the herb is still "wet" or the bag feels damp, take the herbs out, divide them up, and put them in fresh bags.

Hanging: One of the more popular methods of drying herbs is probably the most fun too. The lovely scent of drying plant material can add that witchy feel to a room or space. This is also a great method because you can dry bigger bunches at once and as they are hanging, the air circulates better so you don't have as many issues with moulding. That being said, you do have to make sure you hang them in a room with enough aeration and not a huge abundance of bugs.

STORING HERBS

Once you've dried your herbs, you will need to store them somewhere. This is the fun part, the bit where you can let your creative spirit run wild. I like storing my herbs in recycled glass coffee jars because they are easy to get a hold of, don't cost much, and are the most practical use of space, but nowadays there is such a selection of different kinds of jars, bottles and containers that you can store your herbs however you choose. If you're challenged for space, keeping them in the paper bags is also fine.

I will admit, I am not the most creative when it comes to labelling; I tend to take a more practical approach, so my jars have plain white labels with the herb's common name, Latin name, gender, element, and magical and medicinal uses. Because I also work with purchased bulk herbs, this helps streamline my apothecary and makes a handy reference for making teas, tinctures, ointments, incenses and all manner of herbal delights.

That being said, you don't have to do as I do. There are so many different options – labels that are hand drawn, hand painted, printed on parchment, made in the shape of the plant material, or simply hand written with whatever information you want to include. Just be sure to label them so you know what the plant material is!

Chapter Six: TREES OF THE HEDGE WITCH

The trees are the secret keepers of the land. Within them they hold the lifeblood of above and below. Their roots go deep into the ground, connecting with the energies of the underworld and the earth mother. Their branches and leaves sway in the wind, carrying messages from above to below; the whispers on the wind hold great knowledge if only we would learn to listen. They are the ancient spirits of the land and the guardians of the realm.

Trees are an integral part of daily life. They turn carbon dioxide into oxygen, hold soil together, provide wood, and offer shelter, shade, and homes for a huge assortment of flora and fauna. They are often an eco-system all their own and without trees, civilization would face an unpleasant future. They deserve honor and respect and as such, have found themselves to be the object of worship by many different cultures; the druids held the Oak sacred and would often perform rituals and workings within a grove of Oaks.

There are many different trees that are considered sacred, and entire books have been written on the subject, but to get you started in the lore of trees, here is a short list.

ALDER
(Alnus Glutinosa)

The alder is an old tree, a guardian and connector to other realms, sacred to the Druids. It is a tree of strength and battle, often referred to as the "battle witch"; it will stand tall in the face of adversity. Alder doesn't mind the wet, and because of this tolerance it was used to build roads, fish traps, and other things requiring water resistance.

The alder tree is known to heal many different ailments, including but not limited to inflammation, rheumatism and chronic skin diseases. Alder helps make pathways to the realm of the Fae, so hold an alder in your hand whilst moving into their realm; it is both a key and a gift. The alder often appears to bleed when the bark is cut or scratched, and it was often worshipped and revered for this phenomenon.

It is said that alder holds all four elements within it; this makes it exceptionally powerful. An alder wand would be an amazing magical ally, but one must be careful when holding the elements in their hands during magical workings.

APPLE
(Malus Domestica)

There is nothing quite like the scent of apple blossoms in the spring. It invades the senses, clouding the mind with its sweet, summery aroma. It comforts, yet also heralds a feeling of anticipation for the warmer weather.

The apple is so ingrained in daily life that it is sometimes hard to view with a reverent or mystical perspective. Yet it is a fruit of the Gods, a fruit of the Underworld, a key to knowledge and a spirit of Avalon. The apple holds a pentagram in its center and is the favorite fruit of many.

It is best used at Mabon and Samhain as a symbol of the Harvest and Otherworld. It is also used in love magic, sacred to Venus and Aphrodite. Create a candle of apple scent or luscious apple crumble in reverence to the spirit of this ancient and delicious fruit.

ASH
(Fraxinus Excelsior)

Reputed to be the same type of tree as the great Yggdrasil; the ash is known throughout magical lore. It is sacred to Odin and Woden, the Norse and Briton Gods (Woden is believed to be the naturalized version of Odin in the British Isles). The sacredness of the ash is represented in the saying *"By Oak, Ash and Thorn,"* a blessing to close ritual or spellwork in Druidry.

The main action of the ash is protection, but given its associations with all three worlds (Upper, Middle, Lower) in the form of the World Tree, it could also be used for entering other realms, or "crossing the hedge." A sprig of ash carried in hand whilst performing a crossing would offer protection and also turn away psychic attacks.

BIRCH
(Betula Alba)

The birch is a well-known magical tree used throughout antiquity for rites and rituals of witches and of older societies like the Celts, Germanics, Scandinavians, and Native Americans. The Maypole during Beltane rituals was said to be made from a birch, as is the handle of one of the oldest symbols of a witch, the besom, due to its protective and purifying qualities. It is a flexible tree, often grown in copses to use as firewood as it burns evenly and doesn't pop as some woods do, and the bark would have been a fantastic kindling starter.

Birch also possesses great healing powers. It is a natural diuretic, aiding in cleansing and detoxifying the urinary system; as it has astringent qualities it is also great to help tone and tighten skin and can be used in the treatment of acne.

The birch is associated with water and as such, can be used magically for lunar spells, healing, renewal, rebirth, and the realm of psychic ability and prophecy. Birch is represented by Berkana in the Norse runic alphabet and by Beith in the Celtic ogham alphabet.

BLACKTHORN
(Prunus Spinosa)

On the surface, the blackthorn seems to represent darkness, strife and all sort of nastiness, but beneath the tough exterior of this thorny hedge plant is a powerful spirit; it only has to be found. It is a protective tree, although its associations with the more chaotic should not be discounted.

Irish shillelaghs were made from blackthorn, as were walking sticks used by English witches and blasting rods (or wands). Blackthorn has a prickly nature, but its thorns can be used in protective and poppet magic. The tree gets its name from its black bark. During the winter it can look dead because it loses its leaves and appears to be a twisted stick or skeleton of a tree.

This mysterious tree is associated with winter, the ancient goddesses The Cailleach and The Morrigan, and with the darker aspects of the Craft—the dark phases of the Moon and the Crone. The thorny hedge in Sleeping Beauty was blackthorn; it asked the Prince to prove his worthiness before entering the domain of the sleeping princess. It is a tree that demands sacrifice, but not without reason, and for every individual who works with the blackthorn, the sacrifice and reason will be different.

ELDER
(Sambucus Nigra)

Another great magical tree of antiquity, the elder is incredibly powerful. Its healing properties alone are well known: the flowers and berries are used in various forms to treat flu, cough, and other immune issues. Richly scented flowers bloom in "heads" before giving way to the lush purple berries it is well known for. The berries are perfect for making syrups, tinctures and jams. The flowers are better utilized in a tea or infusion if being taken for treatment; however, the flowers also flavor desserts beautifully, one such dessert being elderflower panna cotta.

It is said that the elder tree holds a spirit of a witch. When one approaches the elder in need of its wood, bark, or other parts, one must always ask for permission by saying *"Old Woman, give me some of thy wood and I will give thee some of mine when I grow into a tree,"* and only take from the tree once permission is given. Otherwise, strife and discord will follow. It is said, in German folklore, that the elder holds the spirit of the Elder Mother or Hyldemor.

Unfortunately throughout its long history, the elder has fallen prey to some rather unsavory tales, such as the one that says the elder is the tree from which Judas hung himself after his betrayal of Christ. (Given how an elder grows and the fact that it is more of a shrub than tree, however, it could be reasoned that it was impossible or at least impractical for Judas to hang himself from an elder.) The elder is also a tree of the Faery; sitting under an elder on Samhain, one may find themselves seeing the Fae.

Bathing your eyes with the dew of this tree will also empower your sight to see faeries and witches.

HAWTHORN
(Crataegus Monogyna)

The Hawthorn is another tree well known throughout antiquity. The Hawthorn blooms with lusciously perfumed white flowers before its blood red berries appear. It is a hedgerow plant and not uncommon to find growing on the side of the road within the company of other hedgerow folk such as elder, dog rose or blackberry. However, the hawthorn can also stand alone as a tree and reach impressive heights if in the right kind of soil. It is the "thorn" in the phrase "by Oak, Ash and Thorn," with impressive thorns that can be used in protective magic and to pierce poppets.

Hawthorn is a Faery tree; the Fae live within the tree as guardian spirits, and are said to punish anyone who offends. It is a tree of fertility and was once referred to as "May," indicating the blossoming of the tree during May, the time in the northern hemisphere when Beltane is celebrated. It was used to promote fertility and happiness in marriage.

As a protective symbol, the hawthorn was often planted to ward off negativity and intentions of the evil kind. It would deflect storms and lightening. Like the elder, it is unwise to remove any part of the tree or shrub without asking the appropriate permissions and appealing to the spirits of the tree. If the tree is inhabited by the Fae this is especially important, as they are not known for suffering fools at all.

OAK
(Quercus Robur)

The ancient sentinel of the woods, the king of trees, a being of strength, power, and long-held wisdom and knowledge, the oak is perhaps one of the most sacred of trees. The Druids held this tree especially sacred, often performing rites and workings within a grove of oaks. An oak's roots are the same size as its canopy, and the size of some oaks can take your breath away. They can reach heights of over 100 feet and have impressive girths of up to thirty feet or more.

Oaks are long lived trees; it is said that some are as old as four hundred years. It is no surprise the oak is considered king, as it holds such majesty. During the later autumn and early winter months when the oak sheds its leaves, take advantage and rake some of them up—they make brilliant mulch and compost.

ROWAN
(Sorbus Aucuparia)

The first woman was made from rowan just as the first man was made from the ash, so Norse legend tells us. She is also known as witchwood, witchbane, and the Lady of the Mountain. She stands proud, her red berries glistening, asking to be used as protective charms against those who would send negative energies or malevolent workings toward you.

It is said faeries would inhabit the rowan, and rowans growing near homes would help protect the people who resided within. Rowan wood can be carried to increase psychic powers; an equal-armed cross made of rowan wood and bound with red thread is known to be a particularly powerful protective amulet. The berries carried in a charm bag aid in luck and success.

SPINDLE
(Euonymus Europaeus)

When one hears of the spindle tree, tales of Sleeping Beauty or the delightfully wicked Rumpelstiltskin may come to mind. Whether it is spinning straw into gold, or a deep sleep caused by a prick to the finger, spindles were considered to be quite magical. The spindle tree also has something of a wicked reputation, as its attractive berries are considered poisonous and have tricked many a child into sampling its darksome delights.

The spindle is a hardwood, which made it perfect for carving into the points for spindles; it is an element of tree magic within the home, work blessed by the spirit of the tree. Hedge witches and weavers past would have used this tree in order to create their own clothes, spin their own wool, and likely make some money doing this kind of work; it would have also been a wonderful tool to help create poppet stuffing.

There is something of an element of trance work involved in spinning; the continued, repetitive, focused action can bring about a shift in thinking and a shift in perception that creates an almost trance-like state. It also brings to mind the Fates – weavers and spinners of fate who hold the future of every being in this world in their hands as well as the Norns who sit below Yggdrasil and carve, spin and weave the fates of those who reside within all the realms.

WILLOW
(Salix Alba)

The willow, how she weeps as she sweeps her branches across the quiet surface of the lake. She is powerfully enchanting and holds herself to some very ancient Goddesses such as Circe, Hecate, and Persephone. She is emotion and water, psychic ability and prophecy. The willow bends but she does not break, showing flexibility in the face of adversity, of knowing when not to stand too firm lest that firmness shift from under you.

A witch's besom is traditionally bound with willow, adding layers of protection, emotion, and heart. The most important compound in aspirin, *salicin,* is found in willow bark. If you have a sensitivity or allergy to aspirin, it is best to avoid willow in herbal preparations.

YEW
(Taxus Baccata

The sentinel of death, the tree of the Underworld, cemetery guardian, immortal: the yew is one of the most sacred trees. It holds the same sacredness of the Oak in many spiritual traditions. It is most often found within cemetery grounds, as it is a funerary tree. It is a symbol of everlasting life, as it is evergreen, lushly presenting its darkly lovely greenery to the world. It is a glorious tree, powerful, mysterious and otherworldly. To stand before the yew is to feel its energy, to feel the pull of the spirit of the tree calling you to understand its ways. It is toxic—make no mistake, it can kill—but it can also call to the darkest parts of your soul and help you realize them to the surface, to bathe them in light and understand the nuances that hide your shadows.

The yew is a symbol of death and rebirth. It has earned this by the strange way it grows. The branches grow into the ground and form new trunks, growing up around the old trunk, almost making it impossible to tell where the old tree started and the new growth began. It is said that the Fortingall Yew in Glen Lyon, Scotland, is well over two thousand years old, and potentially almost nine thousand, showing the immense age that a yew tree can reach.

Yew is the tree for connecting with ancestors, for understanding and connecting with the old magic. It is considered a shamanic tree on account of its connections to the underworld and Otherworld. It heightens psychic ability and personal power. Burning yew will assist in contacting the spirits of the Dead; however, I would recommend doing this outside or in a well-ventilated area on account of the toxicity of yew.

Chapter Seven: TOOLS OF THE HEDGE WITCH

What is a witch without the tools of the trade that help her work her magic? There are many things spoken of in lore that witches would use as aids to cross the hedge, cast magic, and warp reality to bend to their will. In today's witchcraft tradition we have the well-known tools such as an athame, wand, cauldron and chalice—these are tools that have featured heavily in witchcraft since its modern inception.

Hedge witches, while indulging in these classics, will also work with other tools. For example, even though an athame would be handy to help cut through energetic issues when crossing, there are more personal tools that a witch will create in order to help her cross the hedge and remain protected whilst doing so.

The following is by no means a comprehensive list of tools that a hedge witch would use, and other hedge witches would probably add more or subtract a few. This is simply a starting point for you to be able to begin building your toolkit as you grow on your path as a practitioner.

From there you will learn what works best for you, and be able to incorporate it into your journeys over the hedge.

FLYING OINTMENT

There is perhaps no more famous tool of the witch than the flying ointment. It has been enjoying something of a renaissance in modern times, and as hedge witchcraft has become more popular, people are even making and selling it online in varying potencies to the general public. Flying ointments are made with psychoactive herbs that affect the pineal gland (thought to be the third eye), allowing for a trance or dream-like state when awake, thus assisting in crossing the hedge, astral projecting and working with Otherworld.

If you look throughout history, you will see references to the flying ointment, though perhaps under another name such as witch's salve, green salve, lycanthropic ointment, or sabbatic unguent. The famed witch Medea, a student of Hecate and witch of note in the story of Jason and the Argonauts, created an unguent to assist Jason in capturing the Golden Fleece. As a Priestess of Hecate, Medea undoubtedly would have used quite powerful herbs in her unguent.

The flying ointment can also be found in other historical references, such as in *The Golden Ass*, written by Lucius Apuleius in 160AD:

"On a day Fotis came running to me in great fear, and said that her mistress, to work her sorceries on such as she loved, intended the night following to transform herself into a bird, and to fly whither she pleased. Wherefore she willed

me privily to prepare myself to see the same. And when midnight came she led me softly into a high chamber, and bid me look through the chink of a door: where first I saw how she put off all her garments, and took out of a certain coffer sundry kinds of boxes, of the which she opened one, and tempered the ointment therein with her fingers, and then rubbed her body therewith from the sole of the foot to the crown of the head."

—Lucius Apuleius, *The Golden Ass,* Book III, Chapter 16.

Contrary to this example, however, it is important to *not* slather flying ointment on like a cream, especially one made from the baneful herbs; incrementally small doses are the best way to test your reaction. The same recommendation would be given for *any* herbal remedy, ointment, or treatment, regardless of specific ingredient, as one can never predict the effects of herbs on the body.

Ointments are quite simple in structure; they are basically herb-infused oils thickened with wax. In times past, ointments (whether flying or healing) would have been made with a tallow base instead of wax, as wax was not as easily available as it is today. Ointments are one of the easiest and most fun crafts to make, and you'll find a few simple recipes in Chapter 10. However, I would suggest learning more about herbs and their applications before attempting to make a salve that you would be putting on your skin.

TEAS

I am a prolific tea drinker. Nothing gets my day started quite like a strong cup of tea, and I imagine this is probably true for many a witch, whether it be tea or coffee. My tea of choice is English Breakfast, strong with milk; I'll admit, I do prefer the traditional cup of tea and it is often by my side when I am reading tarot cards, as it helps focus my mind and engage the senses.

With the plethora of herbs available in the world, you could design a tea that suits any purpose; even for crossing the hedge. Whilst I would caution against using dangerous or strong psychoactive herbs to help slip your mind into a receptive mood, there are several herbs that can enhance psychic ability, open the third eye, and help the mind enter a trance-like state, perceptive to things not easily seen with the waking eye.

The best way to make tea is to choose herbs that you love to drink and/or think would help you in your quest. Blend them together, put one teaspoon of the blend in a cup, and cover with hot water. Allow it to steep until the desired flavor or depth of color is achieved. Then simply strain the herbs and drink. I like to use a clear glass teapot when I can; this allows me to watch the alchemical process of dried herbs changing to tea. The colors are quite beautiful.

Chamomile
(*Matricaria chamomilla*)

Most would be familiar with chamomile; it is a staple herbal tea in most supermarket aisles. Chamomile has that pungent vanilla-citrus scent that permeates whether fresh, dried, or steeping for tea. It has a long history as a healing herb that relaxes the mind and helps when trying to sleep. Chamomile is an excellent herb in a tea for hedge work; it allows the mind to relax and enter a state of restfulness that can be guided toward lucid dreaming and astral projection experiences.

Cinnamon
(*Cinnamon verum*)

A powerfully warming spice, cinnamon is a wonderful herb to add to any sort of psychic tea, if you observe the idea of moderation. It is strongly flavored and can cause adverse reactions if consumed in large amounts, so I would not recommend drinking a cup of straight cinnamon tea. Instead, add it to other herbs to give a warming sensation and sweet back note.

Damiana
(*Turnera diffusa*)

While this small woody shrub with bright yellow flowers is more often thought of as an aphrodisiac and libido booster, Damiana is also quite a potent psychic ally known to help with lucid dreaming and aiding restlessness. The herb is actually mildly psychoactive, and people have been known to smoke this in lieu of the more famous, yet mostly illegal, *Cannabis sativa* (marijuana). Damiana is an ideal herb to have in a tea to help release the everyday bonds on the mind and allow it to open up psychically.

Jasmine Flower
(*Jasminum officinale*)

Jasmine is one of my most favorite herbs; there is nothing like the scent of blooming jasmine on a warm summer's evening to transport the mind and soul to another place. It is one of the memories that I carry throughout my life, as my family home has a beautiful jasmine vine that flowers quite prolifically. Jasmine has always been a very popular tea ingredient; or at least the scent of jasmine has been. In China, a tea made from green tea leaves and scented with jasmine has been a staple brew for more than five hundred years, showing its longevity and popularity as a favored plant.

Lavender
(*Lavendula angustifolia*)

While the idea of lavender likely brings up country fields, air freshener, or Grandma's perfume, lavender has been used throughout history for all manner of things, from scenting to strewing, to healing and relaxing, for magical work, and as a tea. Lavender is excellent for relaxation, dream recall and to enhance or help psychic ability and dreams.

Mint
(*Mentha spp*)

Mint is one plant that is very easily obtainable, great tasting and refreshing, with a plethora of species including spearmint, peppermint, common mint and catnip (to name but a few—there are also many flavor variations, from chocolate to ginger). While one wouldn't automatically assign it to working with the third eye or hedge crossing, given it is more often associated with money, mint is a great herb to use in clairvoyant teas. It opens the third eye, allows for the mind to relax and also aids in spirit communication.

Mugwort
(*Artemisia vulgaris*)

Mugwort is known to be a potent psychic enhancer and tool to aid in astral projection. Most modern flying ointments contain this herb because of its psychoactive qualities, and while it is a gentler herb that some others discussed in this book, it is still quite powerful. It is a very bitter herb, so will need other herbs and possibly a sweetening additive to make it palatable, but is definitely a good herb to use when trying to achieve trance state and hedge crossing.

(Again, do not use mugwort in any way if you are trying to get pregnant, suspect you are pregnant or are indeed pregnant, as this can bring on menstruation and cause spasms in the uterus. Also do not drink if you are allergic to thujone.)

Rose Petals
(*Rosa centifolia*)

More famous as a potpourri or love herb, rose has its own unique gifts when it comes to psychic ability and accessing other realms. It is a gentle herb, but as you know, rose also has it thorns, which means it can pack a bit of a punch when it wants to. Rose is a staple in my psychic tea of choice; not only does it add a decidedly delicate spray of color, but it also adds a nice floral flavor when mixed with earthier herbs. I have chosen *Rosa centifolia* as the genus here because it is also one of the most strongly scented roses. It also holds its scent for a very long time, so if you were inclined to use it in sachets instead of tea, it would suit perfectly.

Skullcap
(*Scutellaria lateriflora*)

Skullcap, a member of the mint family, is one of the best-known herbs for helping with insomnia next to valerian. It is said that smoking skullcap provides an experience not dissimilar from cannabis sativa, though skullcap is milder and more widely legal. It is a useful herb to help with meditation and opening the pathways in the mind.

Valerian
(*Valeriana officinalis*)

As an earthy herb, valerian is very much connected to the Otherworld. It isn't everyone's cup of tea, given its very pungent scent, but it's been used for millennia to relax, to relieve insomnia, and to connect with animal spirits. Valerian would be a suitable offering and a good tool to assist with relaxing the waking mind into a state that is more receptive to crossing.

Yarrow
(*Achillea millefolium*)

While yarrow doesn't immediately come to the forefront of the mind as an herb to aid in hedge crossing, psychic ability or astral projection, is it quite a good herb to use for these purposes. Not only does it help with prophetic dreaming, cleansing the aura, and protection during divination rites, but it's also fairly neutral taste-wise, so it can help bulk out your herbal tea and create a milder flavor.

TINCTURES

A tincture is a medicinal concoction made with herbs and an alcohol, vinegar, or glycerin base. Tinctures are used in matters of healing, health and in some cases, magic. A tincture is also a great way to preserve herbs, giving them more longevity.

A famous historical example is Four Thieves Vinegar; an antimicrobial tincture that was reputed to have saved the lives of some rather enterprising burglars during the Black Plague. It contained some powerfully antibacterial, antimicrobial and antiseptic herbs, including garlic, rosemary, lavender, meadowsweet, and wormwood. The tincture is still in use today, with many variations on the original recipe commercially available.

What kinds of herbs could be tinctured for hedge crossing? Any of the herbs mentioned in the tea section would work, either as a single note tincture or in combination with one another. Skullcap can help to promote a meditative state, valerian helps relax the mind, and mugwort can help induce astral projection. Try each on their own or try a combination of the three to relax the mind, promote a meditative state, *and* open the mind to be able to receive visions and astral project.

Tinctures are very easy to make. Simply measure out the dried herb and cover it with alcohol; this could be done in a 1:3 ratio (for dried herbs) or 1:2 or even 1:1 for fresh herbs. If using fresh herbs, allow them to wilt and evaporate some of the water before adding them to the alcohol, vinegar, or glycerin. Otherwise you risk creating an environment for botulism.

HEDGE WITCH'S BAG

When you think of a witch, many different images can come to mind, but I always think of the country woman who walks the laneways in her floppy hat whilst collecting different specimens to use in her magical crafts. I see her strolling along, a small leather pouch hanging from her belt; she may touch it or rub it whilst muttering to herself; almost as though it is guiding her on her path. I think of this as the hedge witch's bag—although it has its origins in Druidry as a crane bag, it can be adapted for use in hedge witchcraft.

So what is a hedge witch's bag all about? It is usually a small bag that can be attached to a belt or wrist, or worn around the neck; it could be made from any natural material such as leather, wool, cotton, linen, or animal skin. The purpose of the hedge witch's bag is to hold items that that can be used during your journeys in Otherworld. Think of it as a mini toolkit that you can take with you; it may consist of items that are personally significant to you or representations of your path.

It may hold crystals or gemstones for protection, psychic power and opening roads; rocks or shells from places of power; animal parts such as feathers, fur, claws, teeth or bones (handy if you want to shapeshift into an animal whilst journeying); charms or talismans of power, and herbs, roots or resins that are important to you. This is by no means a comprehensive list; each bag should be personalized to you and what helps fuel your personal power. However, it's a good rule of thumb to keep your hedge bag private and not share the contents with others.

RATTLES AND DRUMS

Rattles and drums are ancient tools of trance and meditation. There is probably not a culture on this earth that hasn't used them in one way or another; you only have to look to the Native Americans, to Siberia, Australia, the African continent, China and the Middle East. Whether it was for ritual, trance, celebration, music making or path working, rattles and drums have been the tool of many a shaman, witch, spiritual practitioner and tribe for millennia.

Drums are powerful tools for shifting consciousness; the rhythmic beat can mimic the heartbeat, the pounding of your blood as it flows through your body. It reaches into the soul and echoes the very heartbeat of Mother Earth herself; when you lose yourself in the beat of the drum, it grabs you by your bones and moves your mind to another place.

Drumming is a fantastic way to shift your perception before hedge crossing. It allows the mind to simply exist within the beat, losing all sense of reality, shifting to another place where Spirit dances, connecting your heart to those who have come before, those who are in your blood and to the Earth and the power she holds.

A rattle is another great tool for moving the mind into a trance state; whilst it creates a different kind of experience than drums, it is still a powerful ritual tool. Rattles have been used around the world in many different cultures, from the Ancient Egyptians who used them in funerary rites to Native Americans who use them in ceremonial dances. In modern times, rattles are used in dances to uplift the spirit and to get the crowd moving (think of maracas).

Rattles are also very easy to make yourself—if you have a container that can hold small hard objects to make the noise, you have a handmade rattle. Varying the internal items can also offer different types of rattle sounds. A very simple, low-cost rattle would be a wooden cylinder filled with small shells or grains.

TALISMANS

As mentioned in Chapter 3, a talisman is an important tool for your hedge crossing journey. A talisman could be a simple pentagram or even a small clay tablet with a runic symbol painted upon it. Another option is the Evil Eye—an ancient talisman used to divert evil intentions or ill wishes against a person. A related ancient symbol, the Hamsa, incorporates the Evil Eye with an open hand; this talisman can be found hanging up in windows to protect the people within the home and the property itself.

If you wanted to be more creative you could make a clay talisman, carved with a rune to represent protection, success, or whatever other aim you have. It can have herbs pressed into it or even personal items so it is more directly tied to you. The possibilities are endless. You could even add your personal talisman to your hedge witch bag to offer additional protection on your journey.

Chapter Eight:
THE HEDGE WITCH'S ALTAR

A witch's altar is her sacred center, whether it is a working altar or devotional space. Altars are living things; they hold their own spirit, so they should be tended as you would a spirit or Deity. A working altar that is looked after, fed, cleaned, and used consistently will begin to hold the energy of your magic and the energy of its spirit, and contribute quite powerfully to the magic you work.

These days, many metaphysical supply shops sell premade altars with intricate and elaborate carvings on top, but you can make an altar out of any flat surface. My first altar top was a big black tile with a pentagram on it that my stepdad patterned using a sandblaster. I still use it to this day. My altar is slightly larger of course, but the tile remains in the center as my "working space," and a safe area to burn candles or incense on.

Your altar should be a reflection of your path and the magic you practice. There is no right way to create an altar. I often recommend that you start with the basics and go from there, adding or subtracting things as you move along your path. Eventually, your personality and tastes will dictate your space and it will be wholly attuned to you.

My first recommendation when setting up an altar – hedge witch or otherwise – is to have a flat surface that is easy for you to sit or kneel at. If you have children or animals who would be quite eager to touch things, then please place your altar higher up where it can't be reached. You can also look at whether or not you want an indoor or outdoor altar, or both, if you have the space.

Below is a list of items that could be used on your altar to aid you on your hedge witchcraft path. It is by no means a comprehensive list, nor should you feel that you need every single item in order to practice. As with all things spiritual. take what suits and works for you and leave what doesn't resonate. Have fun, be creative, and create the hedge witch space that works best for you.

ALTAR COVER

I like to have a covering on my altar. It's a simple black tablecloth, but you can be as simple or as fancy as you like. Metaphysical supply shops often sell an assortment of colorful and patterned altar cloths.

However, if you are going to be burning candles, incense, or herbs on your altar, definitely have a heatproof tile, board, or other surface to do this on. The last thing you want is to have a cloth or other flammable surface set your house on fire. A designated "fire safe" area will also help prevent wax, charcoal, or ash getting on your altar cloth. But always remember, safety first!

STATUARY/DEITY REPRESENTATION

If you have any particular Deities that you work with and would seek guidance from when working, it is a good idea to have a physical representation of them on your altar. There are many stores that have some rather excellent statuary of Deities that could be used to adorn your sacred space.

If you don't work with Deity but feel as though you would like some representation of the Divine on your altar, choose a representation of what Divine means to you. Otherwise, you can opt to have no representation at all on your altar—it is not required.

WORKING SURFACE

As mentioned above, if you choose to have a larger altar and would like to have many different things on it, a working surface that is non-flammable and safe to work on is a must.

My recommendation would be a simple old-fashioned kitchen or bathroom tile. They're usually pretty sturdy, tend not to catch fire and are very easy to clean. You could etch it or pattern it to suit your path so it connects more strongly with you, or you could simply keep it plain, since I imagine it will get quite beat up from use.

ELEMENTAL REPRESENTATIONS

The elements are an important part of the hedge witch's path. They are the fabric that holds the worlds together and the energies that you will tap into when out and about in the wild working your craft. There are many different ways to represent the elements on your altar. The traditional items (bowl of water, bowl of salt, incense stick and candle) are a good place to start, but there are plenty of alternative representations as well:

<u>Air:</u> The mind, the psychic self.
Color: yellow
Direction: east
Representations: athame, censer, sword, feathers, bells, wind chime, or small besom

<u>Earth:</u> the practical physical self.
Color: green (black or brown can also be used)
Direction: south in the Southern Hemisphere, north in the Northern Hemisphere
Representations: gemstones, plants, pentacle, acorns, dirt, or wood chips

<u>Fire:</u> passion, sexuality.
Color: red (can also be orange)
Direction: north in the Southern Hemisphere, south in the Northern Hemisphere
Representations: wand, brass or gold, lamps, dragons blood, LED light or electric flame candle

Water: spirit, our blood, and our intuitive mind.
Color: blue, silver
Direction: west
Representations: cauldron, goblet, mirror, hag stones, shells, dried seaweed

Spirit: As an element, Spirit doesn't necessarily need a representation, as your whole altar will be in service to your work and to Spirit. However, you could still include items that relate to Spirit to you, such as divination tools, a crystal ball, or even a little jar or bottle filled with herbs that represent Spirit.

CAULDRON

Cauldrons are historically one of the quintessential witch's tools. I often use mine to burn loose incense instead of having a censer for that particular use. You can also use them to scry with, brew small batches of tea, create black salt, etc.—they are quite versatile.

Cauldrons also come in many different sizes and types nowadays; you can go with the traditional cast iron one, but there are also painted ceramic ones decorated with different symbols, stainless steel ones and more. If you desire a larger cauldron, a camping supply store would be your best bet, as you can purchase potjie pots and dutch ovens which function beautifully as cauldrons.

STANG

The stang is a tool that evokes images of a wisened old witch walking with the forked stick of wood, conjuring all sort of wonders and magics. With a long history of use in witchcraft, it ties back to times past when our forebears were quietly practicing their Craft in the wooded glades and glens, far from prying eyes.

The traditional stang is a forked piece of wood that represents the Horned God or the Witch Father; it was introduced into modern witchcraft by Robert Cochrane (an English traditional witch) and has become an ingrained part of practice within traditional witchcraft. The main function of the stang, other than as a representation of the Horned God, is to aid in spirit flight, and it can be used as a portable altar.

While it may not be the most practical tool in its full length to use when hedge crossing, a smaller version can be made and placed upon the altar. To this you can add any talismans, charms or amulets that you wish to take with you while journeying. It can be anointed in oils for that purpose, used as a protective item and used functionally to stir your cauldron.

BESOM

"In rifleing the closet of the ladie, they found a pipe of oyntment, wherewith she greased a staffe, upon which she ambled and galloped through thick and thin."

—Raphael Holinshed on Dame Alice Kyteler, from *Chronicle of Ireland* (1587)

Next to the cauldron, the witch's broom, or besom, would have to be the most recognized tool of the witch. A besom operates as a tool to cleanse and purify a space before and after ritual, however it can also be used as a tool for flying.

Historically people believed that witches anointed the staff of their brooms with ointment and rode upon it; it was more likely that the broom and ointment acted as sympathetic magic to represent their astral flight and spirit journeying. Most witches will have their own besom, whether large or small, somewhere within the house, and often near the altar (or on it, if it's a small symbolic besom).

Besoms were traditionally made from ash and willow, ash being the staff and willow being the bristles; although other references suggest that the broom head was made from birch and the staff from hawthorn. If making your own besom, you could hunt down traditional woods and trees in order to fashion it (but please be ethical in your choices) or wait until Halloween when they are in abundance in stores and buy one. It depends on your preference as to what you would like to have.

My besom is made from an oak staff and repurposed bristles from a Halloween broom I bought at a cheap shop. And with so many sizes and types, if you are stuck for space, you will be able to buy one that fits snugly in a small space.

TRANCE AIDS

While not a necessity, keeping your trance aids at hand on your altar will keep them infused with your energy and keep them close at hand when working within your space.

If you perform your hedge crossing with your altar in range, it would make sense to have them close at hand ready for use; they are also magical tools in of themselves, holding energy of their own that they share with you when being used.

HEDGE REPRESENTATION

I feel it is a good idea to have an item on your altar that represents the hedge, especially if your altar is indoors, as this maintains a connection with Otherworld. If you are lucky enough to have an outdoor altar, a potted plant of one of the herbs most commonly found in the hedge would be a fantastic connection. As a living plant, it represents the ever-changing and ever-growing skill of a hedge witch and the worlds that she travels.

If you have a naturally well-lit indoor altar, then a small plant can work there also. If you don't feel you could work with a live plant, creating charms or pouches out of herbs that you associate with crossing the hedge would be absolutely perfect as well.

BONES AND SKULLS

Skulls are powerful symbols and tools for use during magic. You will find many a witch who works with the Dead using animal bones, imbued with the spirit of the animal as a familiar or helper spirit. A skull can also be a representation of the Deity you work with; for example you may have a crow or raven skull in honor of the Morrigan or The Cailleachs, a deer skull or antlers for Elen of the Ways or the Horned One. You could possibly even channel the energy of a particular skull to shapeshift when traversing other realms; the possibilities are quite numerous.

Always make sure you obtain your bones and skulls from reputable sources. If you like to collect roadkill, always do so safely and make sure you clean the bones properly. Be aware of the laws in your own country too; here in Australia there are severe restrictions about collecting the bones of native animals.

GREEN MAN/GREEN LADY

The Green Man is a fascinating symbol that has appeared carved in many different cathedrals, churches, pagan temples, and ancient graves stretching throughout history from East to West. The Green Woman appears to have been more of a counter point or balance to the Green Man in later literature, but she is no less important; she is the Fae, the Green Sprites, the rebirthing in nature. The motherly, nurturing energy that is abounds during the springtime.

Not everyone works with Green Man and Green Lady, but I see them as essential spirits of the Green and of Otherworld. As a hedge witch you will be embracing the elements of green work: the herbs that you use, the natural elements that will adorn your altar, the trees that will become sacred to you on your path are all the domain of Green spirits. But representations of the Green Man or Green Lady on your altar are not a necessity, if you don't feel comfortable having them in your space.

CANDLES

It's not a witch's space or an altar if we don't mention candles. I wouldn't advise burning candles while you are in trance and leaving them technically "unattended." However, candles are one of the foundational tools of witchcraft, and even as a hedge witch you will find yourself using them.

For example, some practitioners use tapers made from the herb mullein to facilitate connection with spirits and perform protective and banishing works, as mullein is a spirit herb and an herb of the Otherworld.

Chapter Nine: HEDGE CROSSING RITUAL

Now we are at the most important part: performing a hedge crossing ritual. As a hedge witch, you will often cross the hedge to obtain information, learn your craft, and work with Spirit. This ritual is designed to help you on your first and subsequent journeys. However, this ritual is not the only way. It is simply a starting point and you are free to customize or rework it however you wish to suit your own personal practice.

If you are on a time constraint or don't want to spend too much time hedge riding, an ideal option is to take a timer or alarm and set it for the allowable time you have. I would suggest not using a loud, harsh alarm, but something a little bit gentler so you don't jar yourself into a waking state.

You will need:

- Pen and paper or journal
- Blanket and/or pillow
- Incense/smudge tool

- Alarm or timer
- Any tools/hedge bags you are taking with you
- Offerings for Spirit or Deity
- Trance aid (ointment, drums, tea etc.)
- Food and Drink

THE RITUAL

Smudge or incense yourself and the space you are working in to cleanse yourself of any clinging or negative energy.

Place yourself in a comfortable position on the floor or space you are performing your hedge crossing. You can lie down, sit up or stand. If you are lying down or sitting, use a pillow and a blanket to keep you warm.

Once in a comfortable position, cast a protective circle around the space you will be working in. It can be general, or it can involve the protection of any Deity, ancestors or spirit you work with. I prefer to imagine a glass sphere; a psychic friend once told me that a beam or beacon of light is an instant attractant to spirits and not always the nice variety.

If you prefer to follow the traditional actions of circle casting, please feel free to call in the elements and watchtowers as well.

Invoke a Deity or spirit that works with crossroads, gates or entry points. It is important to acknowledge them and receive their permission before entering Otherworld.

Take the time now to work with your trance aid. If you are working with music, begin to play a steady rhythmic beat, if you are dancing, begin to move and perform your actions. If you are using an ointment, apply to the temples, soles of your feet, over the heart and on your wrist pulse points.

Begin breathing deeply and centering your mind. Take 10 deep slow breaths in and out while holding in your mind the objective you are trying to achieve.

Begin your journey to your entry point. This is the place where you will enter Otherworld. It could be a tree trunk, a cave, a mound, or even simply just a decorative door. Move through it and into Otherworld. Feel the space as you move through it—smell the dampness of the cave or the earthiness of the mound, feel the roughness of the tree trunk. Truly experience it.

Once you have entered Otherworld, look for your animal guide. It should be waiting there for you to assist you in your journey. Your familiar spirits or fetch beasts may also be there with you. I would suggest tasking one with watching over you as you journey so you have some protection for your physical form.

If you are there for a purpose, begin working toward your aim. Allow your guide to show you where you need to go in order to obtain the information you are seeking. If you are familiarizing yourself with Otherworld for future journeys, take your time to explore, understand the layout of the land you are in. Sometimes it is a good experience to just let things happen as they will and let the images, thoughts and sensations come to you.

Once you feel the journey is done, retrace your steps back to your point of entry and slowly begin moving back toward your physical body. Thank your animal guide for its assistance during your journey.

When you arrive at your entry point, thank the guides, gatekeepers, or crossroad spirits that opened the way for you. Ask them to close the gates and leave them the offerings you have brought with you for them.

Take some time when you return from Otherworld to absorb the experience. Let it wash over you and settle in your mind before moving or doing any other actions. Gently allow yourself to return to full consciousness. Thank your familiar spirits and fetches and give them the offerings you have for them — if you feed your familiar spirits or fetches in this way.

Take your pen and paper or journal and begin writing down the things you experienced and saw. If you went for a particular reason such as divination, healing or spell work, write down the answers provided to you whilst journeying.

Consume the food and drink that you have in circle with you. The purpose of this is twofold. You will feel a bit depleted of energy, so this will provide an immediate boost. It also reminds the spirit that you are a physical being, and brings your mind into the present moment to focus on eating and drinking.

Once you have written your notes and eaten your food, take down your circle or protective sphere. This is the final note of your journey and will bring your mind and body back to full consciousness in the present, physical world.

SOME NOTES

When you enter Otherworld remember to always be mindful of the creatures that you come across. Manners are important and you will get further if you remember to be polite and not antagonistic. Spirits don't always have your best interests at heart and they don't always have good intentions.

There are entities that will look at you as food, as energy, as something to prey upon, and will have no hesitation in doing so. They will attach themselves to you and try and hitch a ride back. I recommend putting good protections in place when you journey, because you do not know what you will meet on the other side.

The tools you take with you into the circle can be used in Otherworld; they are the physical representation with you that you take on your hedge riding experiences.

Take your time with your experience; it isn't a race. You will learn more and get more from the crossing if you simply take a moment to absorb every bit of information you come across.

If you feel unsafe performing this ritual alone, you can adapt it for two people. The second person can be your anchor and bring you back if things get a little too scary or murky. This ritual can also be adapted for a group setting.

The steps are only an outline and the ritual itself is not overly detailed so as not to influence your experience. Every journey should be tailored to you and what you need to get out of it. This ritual can be adapted and customized to suit your purpose and needs, so please do not feel you must follow it to the absolute letter.

Chapter Ten: CHARMS AND RECIPES OF THE HEDGE WITCH

Let's get our hands dirty and get into some really practical hands-on witchery. Part of being a hedge witch is working with natural elements and creating your own ointments, oils, charms and more—and let's be honest—it's one of the more fun parts of being a witch.

This chapter has some easy recipes for you to try on your own. This is just to get you started; once you begin crafting your own remedies, you will be able to put together new and exciting ones. So have fun, enjoy, and get crafting!

OINTMENTS

Ointments are a simple and fun craft and can assist you in your hedge crossing journeys. They can be put together relatively easily and quickly (allowing for setting time).

A few pointers when creating ointments:

— If you have harvested herbs fresh to use in an ointment, allow them to wilt for a couple of days to let the water evaporate. Water and oil do not mix, and allowing water to end up in the base of your ointment can turn it rancid, breed bacteria, and give you botulism.

— If a recipe calls for fresh herbs but you're using dried, always halve the amount called for, unless you want your ointment to be super concentrated.

— Some like to add essential oils to ointments for added aromatic effect. If you choose to use an essential oil in place of any herbs listed here, be sure to consult trusted sources for instructions and advice. Remember that essential oils can be harmful to the skin and olfactory senses, so research carefully before deciding to include them, and start with very small amounts. In case you have any allergies or sensitivities, patch test any ointment you make by putting a small amount on the skin and leave for 24 hours. (The same can be said of herbs – dried or fresh – always make sure you know your allergies.) If there is no irritation, reaction or inflammation, then the herbs/oils are most likely quite safe for you to use on your skin.

— Common carrier oils for herbal ointments include olive, sweet almond, jojoba, avocado, and grapeseed oils. Use what you have on hand, or experiment with different carriers to find the one you like best.

— You can lessen or increase the amount of beeswax depending on your personal preference for consistency in ointments. If you are vegan, substitute the beeswax with candelilla or carnauba wax (both derived from trees).

Note: I have chosen to not include recipes for traditional or baneful herbal ointments because only experienced herbalists or plant enthusiasts should even consider experimenting with them. If you are curious about simply for knowledge's sake, there are a plethora of recipes available on the internet.

That being said, both wormwood and mugwort contain a compound called *Thujone* so if you have an allergy to it, please do not attempt these ointment recipes. Please be aware when using wormwood/mugwort based salves in general, especially if you are allergic to any plants in the *Asteraceae* family (for example, ragweed). And of course, please do not use if you are pregnant or breast feeding, and if you are taking any medication or suffer from any neurological disorders, please check with your doctor before using.

SIMPLE OINTMENT RECIPE

You will need:

- ¼ cup wax pastilles
- 1 cup carrier oil of choice
- ½ cup dried herbs in proportions of your choice

Instructions:

1. Place herbs and oil in a bain marie (or double boiler)

2. Slowly and gently infuse the herbs into the oil for 40 mins to an hour, or until desired color is reached. Be careful and watch your heat as the herbs can scorch.

3. Strain the herbs out of the oil (can be done hot or at room temperature.)

4. Return the oil mix to the bain marie. (Heat slowly if the oil has cooled.)

5. Add wax pastilles, stirring occasionally until dissolved.

6. Pour ointment mixture into sterilized jars or tins and allow to set before sealing with lids.

Side Note: *An alternative to a double boiler is using a slow cooker on the warm setting in a sealed jar surrounded by a water bath. It does still have to be monitored to make sure the water doesn't dry up but is a less labour-intensive option than stove top.*

Non-Toxic Flying Ointment #1:

- ¼ cup wax pastilles
- 1 cup oil of choice
- ½ cup dried mugwort, vervain, lavender

Non-Toxic Flying Ointment #2:

- ¼ cup wax pastilles
- 1 cup carrier oil of choice
- ½ cup dried wormwood, dittany of Crete, rose petals

Non-Toxic Flying Ointment #3:

- ¼ cup wax pastilles
- 1 cup carrier oil of choice
- ½ cup dried wormwood, mugwort*

*This recipe can also double as a topical pain relief salve, but avoid using if pregnant.

Protection Salve:

- ¼ cup wax pastilles
- 1 cup carrier oil of choice
- ½ cup dried agrimony, juniper, rosemary

Psychic Sight Salve:

- ¼ cup wax pastilles
- 1 cup carrier oil of choice
- ½ cup dried mugwort, rose petals, jasmine flower, eyebright

CHARM BAGS

Charm bags are very useful tools to have with you on your journeys. The basic instructions for creating a charm bag are as follows:

Place your items in the small bag or pouch. Hold the charm between your hands and imagine its purpose in your mind. Speak to it and share with it the purpose for which it has been created. Pass it through the incense three times, then anoint each corner and the center of the charm bag with your protection oil. Recite the appropriate words over your charm bag (see individual recipes below). Make sure you regularly feed your charm bag to keep the energy and intentions fresh.

Charm Bag for Safe Travel:

- Small pouch or organza bag
- Tourmaline tumble stone or chips
- Small key and lock charm
- Bay leaf
- Sprig of rosemary
- Sage leaves
- Protection oil of your choice
- Incense associated with protection

Recite over your bag:

"With these breaths, I give you life. With this oil, I anoint you. With this incense, I consecrate you to ensure safe travels and the protection of my spirit while I journey."

Charm Bag for Spirit Communication:

- Small bag or pouch
- Selenite or tumble stone or chips
- Skull charm or bead piece
- Marshmallow root
- Mugwort
- Dandelion root
- Spirit oil of your choice
- Incense associated with spirit communication

Recite over your bag:

"With these breaths, I give you life. With this oil, I anoint you. With this incense, I consecrate you to allow communication between myself and the realm of Spirit—to hear, speak and understand those who stand beyond, wishing to share their messages."

INCENSES AND SMOKES

The following recipes are ratios only, so that you can determine how big you want your batch of incense to be. Always use care when burning incense.

Protection Incense:

- 2 parts copal resin
- 1 part agrimony
- 1 part angelica
- 1 part fennel
- 1 part juniper

Spirit Incense:

- 2 parts gum arabic resin
- 1 part wormwood*
- 1 part marshmallow root
- 1 part dandelion root, leaf or flower
- 1 part mullein

Burn in a well-ventilated space

Psychic Sight Incense:

- 2 parts dragon's blood resin
- 2 parts mugwort
- 1 part yarrow
- 1 part rose

Hedge Incense:

- 2 parts opoponax resin
- 2 parts elderberry
- 1 part hawthorn leaf/flower/berry
- 1 part mugwort
- 1 part skullcap

World Tree Incense:

- 2 parts benzoin resin
- 1 part sandalwood
- 2 parts oak leaf
- 1 part ash leaf or keys
- 1 part birch

Hedge Crosser's Smoke:*

- 2 parts damiana
- 1 part mullein
- ½ part skullcap
- ¼ part mugwort
- ¼ part motherwort
- ¼ part peppermint

This herbal blend can be used as an incense or smoked like tobacco. Please observe all proper precautions when choosing to inhale any herb into your lungs. Use this blend in a pipe, tobacco rolling papers or vaporizers.

OILS

The recipes below are for oils that can aid you in your hedge witchcraft practice. The formulations are in ratios rather than exact amounts, so you can tailor the recipe according to how much oil you want to make.

Note that these recipes have been formulated with the intention of infusing dried herbs into a carrier oil. The formulations are *not* suitable for use with essential oils. If you choose to use an essential oil in place of any herbs listed here, be sure to consult trusted sources for instructions and advice. As noted earlier, essential oils can be harmful to the skin and olfactory senses, so research carefully before deciding to include them, and start with very small amounts.

In case you have any allergies or sensitivities, patch test any oil blend you make by putting a small amount on the skin and leave for 24 hours. (The same can be said of herbs – dried or fresh – always make sure you know your allergies.) If there is no irritation, reaction or inflammation, then the herbs/oils are most likely quite safe for you to use on your skin.

Common carrier oils for herbal blends include olive, sweet almond, jojoba, avocado, and grapeseed oils. Many people recommend a ratio of 1 part herbs to 5 parts carrier oil, but you can use more or less oil, depending on how potent you want the infusion to be.

Protection Oil:

- 1pt Horehound
- ½ pt Hyssop
- 1 pt Nettle
- 1pt Pine
- 1pt Rosemary

Hedge Crosser's Oil:

- 1pt Wormwood
- 1pt Mugwort
- ½ pt Jasmine
- ½ pt Elder flower
- ¼ pt Blackthorn bark

Psychic Visions Oil:

- 1pt Rose petals
- ½ pt Cinnamon
- ½ pt Honeysuckle
- 1pt Thyme
- 1pt Yarrow

Spirit Work Oil:

- ½ pt Dandelion root
- 1pt Wormwood
- 1pt Mullein
- ¼ pt Poppy
- ½ pt Sandalwood

World Tree Oil:

- 1pt Oak leaf
- 1pt Birch leaf
- 1pt Willow bark
- ¼ pt Pine needles
- ¼ Pt Eucalyptus

BATH SALTS

When you hedge cross, you collect energy in your auric field and within yourself that needs to be cleansed away, and baths are fantastic purification tools.

If you don't have a bathtub, you can mix the bath salts in a bowl with water and pour it over you in your shower (or outdoors). Or, put them in an organza or muslin bag and tie it to your shower head, letting it wash over you. If you want to store the bath salts long-term, use dried herbs rather than fresh.

Basic Bath Salts Recipe:

- 3 parts salt (I like pink Himalayan, but regular salt will do)
- 2 parts Epsom salts
- ½ to 1 part baking soda

Cleansing Bath Salts:

- 3 parts Basic Bath Salts Recipe
- ¼ part hyssop
- ¼ part lemongrass
- ¼ part sage
- ¼ part wood betony

Hedge Crosser's Bath:

- 3 parts Basic Bath Salts Recipe
- ¼ part rose petals
- ¼ part rosehip
- ¼ part jasmine
- ¼ part mugwort

BLESSINGS AND INVOCATIONS

Here are examples of what you can say when approaching the spirits of your ancestors and your animal guides. Over time, you will likely tailor the wording to your own style of practice.

Ancestor Blessing:

"I call upon those of my line and welcome into my space the ancestors who have benevolent intentions and wish only to see the best for me. I invite you into this space to accept my offerings, to visit within this space and commune with your descendant. I am the blood of your blood, the culmination of your dreams, wishes and lives. Please stand with me in this space, guide my hand and guard my spirit as I walk through this world. Ancestors be welcome, eat, drink, take part of this altar and be well."

Animal Guide Invocation:

"By the powers of Earth, Air, Water and Fire
I call to my side my animal guide.
May it be tooth, claw or bone,
Borne of root, leaf or stone,
Please reveal yourself to me,

*So I may see what you shall be.
By all the power that is within,
Let our relationship of Spirit begin."*

CONCLUSION

It has been quite the journey, hasn't it? We've covered quite a lot of information. If you have come to the end of this book and decided that being a hedge witch is not for you, I hope it has at least offered some new ideas or insights that you are able to incorporate into your spiritual path. On the flip side, if you have decided that hedge witchcraft is for you, then I hope that from here, you'll find the way to create your own meaningful, powerful practice that compliments your life and strengthens your connection to your Craft and the natural world.

Hedge witchcraft is such a beautiful and empowering path, but it does require commitment on your part, especially when it comes to learning to cross. It is not an art you will perfect in a short space of time, but it will come easier as you learn and practice more. You will find out what works best for you and go with it.

When you walk the path of the witch, you sometimes find yourself walking it alone; even more so as a hedge witch when your eyes, mind and spirit are constantly walking in two worlds. You will find strength and purpose on this path, opening doors to abilities and worlds you hadn't dreamed of. Otherworld is a place of many possibilities—every time you journey you may just find something different. All it takes is that first step. Good luck and safe travels!

SUGGESTIONS FOR FURTHER READING

While this book has given a good starting point for following the path of the hedge witch, it is always a good idea to read other points of view, do your own research, and form your own opinions. To this end, here is a list of further reading on several topics covered in this book.

Hedge Witchcraft:

To Fly By Night: The Craft of the Hedgewitch. Edited by Veronica Cummer. Pendraig Publishing, 2010.

Hedge Rider. Eric De Vries. Pendraig Publishing, 2008

Pagan Portals – Hedge Riding. Harmonia Saille. John Hunt Publishing, 2012

Cunning Folk and Familiar Spirits: Shamanistic Visionary Traditions in Early Modern British Witchcraft and Magic. Emma Wilby Sussex. Academic Press, 2006

The Hedge Druid's Craft: An Introduction to Walking Between the Worlds of Wicca, Witchcraft and Druidry. Joanna van der Hoeven. Moon Books, 2018.

Herbal Magic and Herbalism:

Cunningham's Encyclopedia of Magical Herbs. Scott Cunningham. Llewellyn Publications, 1985.

Traditional Witchcraft for Fields and Hedgerows. Melusine Draco. Moon Books, 2012.

Rosemary Gladstar's Medicinal Herbs: A Beginner's Guide: 33 Healing Herbs to Know, Grow, and Use. Rosemary Gladstar. Storey Publishing, 2012.

By Wolfsbane & Mandrake Root: The Shadow World Of Plants And Their Poisons. Melusine Draco. Moon Books, 2017.

Witchcraft Medicine: Healing Arts, Shamanic Practices, and Forbidden Plants. Claudia Müller-Ebeling, Christian Rätsch, Wolf-Dieter Storl. Inner Traditions, 2003.

The Witching Herbs: 13 Essential Plants and Herbs for Your Magical Garden. Harold Roth. Weiser Books, 2017.

ABOUT THE AUTHORS

Stacey Carroll is a green path hedge witch, certified herbalist, mad gardener, initiated High Priestess, book lover, and divination enthusiast. Her articles have been published in *Witches and Pagans Magazine*, *The Crooked Path Journal*, *Book of Spells Witches' Planner*, and the now-defunct *Australian Pagan Magazine*. A country girl with a bent sense of humor and a passion for her cats, she has been walking the twisted roads of the witch for many a year now. You can usually find her in the garden, with a book in hand, or in the kitchen baking, loving the life of a country witch and herbalist. Her blog, *The Country Witch's Cottage,* can be found at **www.thecountrywitchscottage.com**

Lisa Chamberlain is the successful author of more than twenty books on Wicca, divination, and magical living, including *Wicca Book of Herbal Spells*, *Wicca for Beginners*, *Runes for Beginners, Elemental Magic,* and *Magic and the Law of Attraction*. As an intuitive empath, she has been exploring Wicca, magic, and other esoteric traditions since her teenage years. Her spiritual journey has included a traditional solitary Wiccan practice as well as more eclectic studies across a wide range of belief systems. Lisa's focus is on positive magic that promotes self-empowerment for the good of the whole. You can find out more about her and her work at her website, **www.wiccaliving.com**.

THREE FREE AUDIOBOOKS PROMOTION

Don't forget, you can now enjoy **three audiobooks completely free of charge** when you start a free 30-day trial with Audible.

If you're new to the Craft, *Wicca Starter Kit* contains three of Lisa's most popular books for beginning Wiccans. You can download it for free at:

www.wiccaliving.com/free-wiccan-audiobooks

Or, if you're wanting to expand your magical skills, check out *Spellbook Starter Kit,* with three collections of spellwork featuring the powerful energies of candles, colors, crystals, mineral stones, and magical herbs. Download over 150 spells for free at:

www.wiccaliving.com/free-spell-audiobooks

Members receive free audiobooks every month, as well as exclusive discounts. And, if you don't want to continue with Audible, just remember to cancel your membership. You won't be charged a cent, and you'll get to keep your books!

Happy listening!

MORE BOOKS BY LISA CHAMBERLAIN

Wicca for Beginners: A Guide to Wiccan Beliefs, Rituals, Magic, and Witchcraft

Wicca Book of Spells: A Book of Shadows for Wiccans, Witches, and Other Practitioners of Magic

Wicca Herbal Magic: A Beginner's Guide to Practicing Wiccan Herbal Magic, with Simple Herb Spells

Wicca Book of Herbal Spells: A Book of Shadows for Wiccans, Witches, and Other Practitioners of Herbal Magic

Wicca Candle Magic: A Beginner's Guide to Practicing Wiccan Candle Magic, with Simple Candle Spells

Wicca Book of Candle Spells: A Book of Shadows for Wiccans, Witches, and Other Practitioners of Candle Magic

Wicca Crystal Magic: A Beginner's Guide to Practicing Wiccan Crystal Magic, with Simple Crystal Spells

Wicca Book of Crystal Spells: A Book of Shadows for Wiccans, Witches, and Other Practitioners of Crystal Magic

Tarot for Beginners: A Guide to Psychic Tarot Reading, Real Tarot Card Meanings, and Simple Tarot Spreads

Runes for Beginners: A Guide to Reading Runes in Divination, Rune Magic, and the Meaning of the Elder Futhark Runes

Wicca Moon Magic: A Wiccan's Guide and Grimoire for Working Magic with Lunar Energies

Wicca Wheel of the Year Magic: A Beginner's Guide to the Sabbats, with History, Symbolism, Celebration Ideas, and Dedicated Sabbat Spells

Wicca Kitchen Witchery: A Beginner's Guide to Magical Cooking, with Simple Spells and Recipes

Wicca Essential Oils Magic: A Beginner's Guide to Working with Magical Oils, with Simple Recipes and Spells

Wicca Elemental Magic: A Guide to the Elements, Witchcraft, and Magical Spells

Wicca Magical Deities: A Guide to the Wiccan God and Goddess, and Choosing a Deity to Work Magic With

Wicca Living a Magical Life: A Guide to Initiation and Navigating Your Journey in the Craft

Magic and the Law of Attraction: A Witch's Guide to the Magic of Intention, Raising Your Frequency, and Building Your Reality

Wicca Altar and Tools: A Beginner's Guide to Wiccan Altars, Tools for Spellwork, and Casting the Circle

Wicca Finding Your Path: A Beginner's Guide to Wiccan Traditions, Solitary Practitioners, Eclectic Witches, Covens, and Circles

Wicca Book of Shadows: A Beginner's Guide to Keeping Your Own Book of Shadows and the History of Grimoires

Modern Witchcraft and Magic for Beginners: A Guide to Traditional and Contemporary Paths, with Magical Techniques for the Beginner Witch

FREE GIFT REMINDER

Just a reminder that Lisa is giving away an exclusive, free spell book as a thank-you gift to new readers!

Little Book of Spells contains ten spells that are ideal for newcomers to the practice of magic, but are also suitable for any level of experience.

Read it on read on your laptop, phone, tablet, Kindle or Nook device by visiting:

www.wiccaliving.com/bonus

DID YOU ENJOY *HEDGE WITCHCRAFT*?

Thanks so much for reading this book! I know there are many great books out there about Wicca, so I really appreciate you choosing this one.

If you enjoyed the book, I have a small favor to ask—would you take a couple of minutes to leave a review for this book on Amazon?

Your feedback will help me to make improvements to this book, and to create even better ones in the future. It will also help me develop new ideas for books on other topics that might be of interest to you. Thanks in advance for your help!